Mastering ServiceNow Scripting

Leverage JavaScript APIs to perform client-side and server-side scripting on ServiceNow instances

Andrew Kindred

BIRMINGHAM - MUMBAI

Mastering ServiceNow Scripting

Commissioning Editor: Gebin George
Acquisition Editor: Heramb Bhavsar
Content Development Editor: Devika Battike
Technical Editor: Prachi Sawant
Copy Editors: Safis Editing, Dipti Mankame
Project Coordinator: Judie Jose
Proofreader: Safis Editing
Indexer: Rekha Nair
Graphics: Tom Scaria
Production Coordinator: Nilesh Mohite

First published: February 2018

Production reference: 1260218

Published by Packt Publishing Ltd.
Livery Place
35 Livery Street
Birmingham
B3 2PB, UK.

ISBN 978-1-78862-709-2

www.packtpub.com

`mapt.io`

Mapt is an online digital library that gives you full access to over 5,000 books and videos, as well as industry leading tools to help you plan your personal development and advance your career. For more information, please visit our website.

Why subscribe?

- Spend less time learning and more time coding with practical eBooks and Videos from over 4,000 industry professionals

- Improve your learning with Skill Plans built especially for you

- Get a free eBook or video every month

- Mapt is fully searchable

- Copy and paste, print, and bookmark content

PacktPub.com

Did you know that Packt offers eBook versions of every book published, with PDF and ePub files available? You can upgrade to the eBook version at www.PacktPub.com and as a print book customer, you are entitled to a discount on the eBook copy. Get in touch with us at service@packtpub.com for more details.

At www.PacktPub.com, you can also read a collection of free technical articles, sign up for a range of free newsletters, and receive exclusive discounts and offers on Packt books and eBooks.

Contributors

About the author

Andrew Kindred moved on to ServiceNow from his background as a programmer and now has over 6 years' experience working with ServiceNow in a range of industry sectors including finance, government, and media.

He is a certified ServiceNow implementation specialist and application developer, currently working in investment banking in London, overseeing and developing implementations and customizations of ServiceNow.

I would like to thank my wife, Holly, for all her support and encouragement, and keeping me well fed while writing. For keeping me motivated and entertained, I would like to thank my daughter Emily. Finally, my thanks to the team at Packt for all their help during the production process.

About the reviewer

Nabil Oukelmoune is a solution architect, an SME with multiple awards in several business areas, an expert in providing IT services and solutions, and is also developing new and innovative processes for many clients across EMEA, the USA, and Asia.

He graduated with honors from the IIHEM with a BBA majoring in management information systems. He has more than 9 years of proven achievements in IT&S including infrastructure management, multi-tiered technical support, process analysis, pm, and solution and enterprise architecture.

Special thanks has to go to the love of my life, queen of my world, and future mother of my kids—my wife, Hajar Ismaili Alaoui. Without you believing in me and nurturing my soul, mind, and tummy, none of this would have been possible—at least not up to this standard of quality and devotion in this little book.

Packt is searching for authors like you

If you're interested in becoming an author for Packt, please visit `authors.packtpub.com` and apply today. We have worked with thousands of developers and tech professionals, just like you, to help them share their insight with the global tech community. You can make a general application, apply for a specific hot topic that we are recruiting an author for, or submit your own idea.

Table of Contents

Preface

ServiceNow is gradually evolving as the platform of choice for IT Service management. Industry giants such as RedHat and NetApp have adopted ServiceNow for their operational needs. ServiceNow provides clients with an extra add-on when it comes to their baseline instances, as scripting can be used to customize and improve the performance of their instances. ServiceNow provides inbuilt JavaScript API for scripting and improving an instance using JavaScript.

This book will initially cover the basics of ServiceNow scripting and the appropriate time to script in a ServiceNow environment. Then, we will dig deeper into client-side and server-side scripting using JavaScipt API. We will also cover advanced concepts such as on-demand functions, script actions, and best practices. This book will act as an end-to-end guide to writing, testing, and debugging scripts in ServiceNow. We will also cover update sets for moving customizations between ServiceNow instances, Jelly scripts for making custom pages, and best practices for all types of script in ServiceNow.

At the end of this book, you will have hands-on experience of scripting in ServiceNow using the inbuilt JavaScript API.

Who this book is for

This book is targeted toward ServiceNow administrators or any stakeholder willing to learn inbuilt JavaScript APIs used to script and customize ServiceNow instances. Experience of working with ServiceNow is mandatory.

What this book covers

Chapter 1, *Getting Started*, introduces you to the basics of ServiceNow scripts. That is, when/why it is appropriate to develop custom functionality through scripting. It also introduces when to configure and customize.

Chapter 2, *Exploring the ServiceNow Glide Class*, provides you with the details of how ServiceNow has exposed its JavaScript APIs, which enables you to write your scripts conveniently. Using these exposed APIs, you can perform various database operations. You will explore some of the commonly used server-side glide classes and client-side glide classes.

Chapter 3, *Introduction to Client-Side Sripting*, helps you understand the client-side scripting of ServiceNow. You will learn about the concepts of client scripts and UI policies. You will see how to write and test basic client-side scripts. You will go through some practical examples of client-side scripting to have better understanding of the functionality.

Chapter 4, *Advanced Client-Side Scripting*, will help you understand the more advanced side of client-side scripting in ServiceNow. You will learn about AJAX calls and UI actions. You will go through some advanced practical examples of client-side scripting to get a better understanding of the functionality.

Chapter 5, *Introduction to Server-Side Scripting*, covers the details of server-side scripting in ServiceNow. It will help you understand the concepts of business rules, UI actions, and access controls in depth. You will also learn how to write and test a server-side script. You will go through some of the practical examples of server-side scripting to understand the functionality better.

Chapter 6, *Advanced Server-Side Scripting*, will cover the advanced side of server-side scripting in ServiceNow. It will help you understand the concepts of script includes, background scripts, workflow scripts, and scheduled jobs. You will go through some practical examples of advanced server-side scripting to understand script calls, the system scheduler, and queuing events in the system.

Chapter 7, *Introduction to Custom Pages*, introduces you to Jelly. This will provide an insight into how Jelly is used in ServiceNow. You will also learn how to create a UI page using JavaScript with Jelly scripting.

Chapter 8, *Scripting with Jelly*, further progresses knowledge of Jelly. This will provide further insight into how Jelly scripting is used in ServiceNow. You will also learn how to create UI Macros to enhance a UI page.

Chapter 9, *Debugging the Script*, introduces the mechanism of debugging your script in ServiceNow. You will explore the various tools and methods used in troubleshooting and debugging your code in ServiceNow.

Chapter 10, *Best Practices*, covers various best practices developers should follow to use ServiceNow in an efficient manner. It also talks about logging and monitoring system performance to control your ServiceNow environment.

Chapter 11, *Deployments with the Update Sets*, guides you on how to move your configurations and customizations from instance to instance. It also helps you understand how to use update sets while working on global and scoped applications. You will also learn how to avoid some common pitfalls while working with update sets.

Chapter 12, *Building a Custom Application Using ServiceNow Scripting*, provides you with an end-to-end implementation of scripting in ServiceNow. You will learn how to build a custom application using scripting provided by ServiceNow.

To get the most out of this book

Before starting with Mastering ServiceNow Scripting, it is advised that you have a good understanding of the ServiceNow platform. It is advisable to have a system administrator certification or similar knowledge, and to be aware of forms, lists, and tables in ServiceNow. You should also be able to comfortably navigate around a ServiceNow instance.

Some knowledge of JavaScript will be advantageous, but is not compulsory as the examples given will give you script to try and get started with.

It is advised to have a ServiceNow instance that you can use to try out the examples and create some scripts of your own. If you do not have an instance at this point, personal developer instances (PDI's) can be requested from ServiceNow for users who would like to improve their ServiceNow skills.

Download the example code files

You can download the example code files for this book from your account at www.packtpub.com. If you purchased this book elsewhere, you can visit www.packtpub.com/support and register to have the files emailed directly to you.

You can download the code files by following these steps:

1. Log in or register at www.packtpub.com.
2. Select the **SUPPORT** tab.
3. Click on **Code Downloads & Errata**.
4. Enter the name of the book in the **Search** box and follow the onscreen instructions.

Once the file is downloaded, please make sure that you unzip or extract the folder using the latest version of:

- WinRAR/7-Zip for Windows
- Zipeg/iZip/UnRarX for Mac
- 7-Zip/PeaZip for Linux

The code bundle for the book is also hosted on GitHub at `https://github.com/ PacktPublishing/Mastering-ServiceNow-Scripting`. In case, there's an update to the code, it will be updated on the existing GitHub repository.

We also have other code bundles from our rich catalog of books and videos available at `https://github.com/PacktPublishing/`. Check them out!

Download the color images

We also provide a PDF file that has color images of the screenshots/diagrams used in this book. You can download it here: `https://www.packtpub.com/sites/default/files/ downloads/MasteringServiceNowScripting_ColorImages.pdf`.

Conventions used

There are a number of text conventions used throughout this book.

`CodeInText`: Indicates code words in text, database table names, folder names, filenames, file extensions, pathnames, dummy URLs, user input, and Twitter handles. Here is an example: "The `onLoad` client script type runs script when a form is loaded."

A block of code is set as follows:

```
function onChange(control, oldValue, newValue, isLoading, isTemplate) {
    if (isLoading || newValue === '') {
        return;
    }

    //Type appropriate comment here, and begin script below

}
```

Bold: Indicates a new term, an important word, or words that you see onscreen. For example, words in menus or dialog boxes appear in the text like this. Here is an example: "To access the studio navigate to **System Applications** | **Studio**. "

 Warnings or important notes appear like this.

 Tips and tricks appear like this.

Get in touch

Feedback from our readers is always welcome.

General feedback: Email `feedback@packtpub.com` and mention the book title in the subject of your message. If you have questions about any aspect of this book, please email us at `questions@packtpub.com`.

Errata: Although we have taken every care to ensure the accuracy of our content, mistakes do happen. If you have found a mistake in this book, we would be grateful if you would report this to us. Please visit `www.packtpub.com/submit-errata`, selecting your book, clicking on the Errata Submission Form link, and entering the details.

Piracy: If you come across any illegal copies of our works in any form on the Internet, we would be grateful if you would provide us with the location address or website name. Please contact us at `copyright@packtpub.com` with a link to the material.

If you are interested in becoming an author: If there is a topic that you have expertise in and you are interested in either writing or contributing to a book, please visit `authors.packtpub.com`.

Reviews

Please leave a review. Once you have read and used this book, why not leave a review on the site that you purchased it from? Potential readers can then see and use your unbiased opinion to make purchase decisions, we at Packt can understand what you think about our products, and our authors can see your feedback on their book. Thank you!

For more information about Packt, please visit `packtpub.com`.

Disclaimer

The code supplied in this book is for use in development scenarios to further knowledge of ServiceNow scripting. Use of the code provided in this book is at the readers own discretion. The author and publisher are not responsible and do not accept liability for any damages or negative impacts brought about from any code used from this book.

1
Getting Started

Welcome. In this book, I hope to teach you and enhance your ServiceNow scripting to ensure you can really be a scripting master. I will show when to configure and when to customize ServiceNow with scripts to achieve your goals. Building on the glide classes of ServiceNow, client- and server-side scripting will also be explored and explained.

Advancing through Jelly script and custom pages, this book also looks at debugging and best practices, rounding off with how to build your own custom applications.

Starting off in this first chapter, we look at when it is appropriate to script, and why scripting should be used, as well as configuring or customizing a ServiceNow instance. We will also explore the basic types of scripts in ServiceNow and when they are run. This chapter also covers the running order of ServiceNow scripts, a brief introduction to scripting, and the script editor used for scripting.

The topics we will cover in this chapter are:

- Configuration versus customization
- When to script in ServiceNow
- Script types
- Order of execution of scripts in ServiceNow
- Basics of scripting
- Script editor

Configuration versus customization

ServiceNow instances are complex. There are a great many ways in which they can be changed, and often, there are several ways to achieve the same goal using different techniques. These changes can be done through configuration and customization.

Configuration uses the ServiceNow interface to set up rules, conditions, and other configurations, like global system properties and filters. This is often made by using a series of drop-down lists.

We can see an example of this in a business rule as follows:

Figure 1.1: Configuration example from a business rule

In *Figure 1.1* we can see filter conditions and and the values to set based on the filter. This configuration example uses no code and is preferable to customization. This type of filtering is seen across the ServiceNow platform.

Most system administrators will be able to administer their instance with configuration alone. A configured instance will suffice for a certain level of functionality on an instance, and, if you are trying to achieve a goal where configuration is available, it is usually the best option.

Customization is when an administrator uses scripts to allow an instance to perform further tasks beyond what configuration can do alone. ServiceNow is extremely open-ended, and the ability to write scripts at multiple points when loading and submitting forms makes it very versatile.

A customization might be to write a script to add a date validation on a field and show a message or clear the field if an incorrect value is entered. Custom scripts are to be managed by the creator, as ServiceNow is not responsible for the code. Therefore, if you start to move into the customization route, make sure you know what you are doing.

As the creator will need to maintain the script created, they will also need to ensure that it will still function when an instance of ServiceNow is upgraded.

If customizing an existing ServiceNow script, rather than customizing the script itself, copy it, rename the copied script, and deactivate the existing script. Then you can make as many changes to the new copied script as you like, while having the original backed up in case it is needed.

To script or not to script?

For new administrators, it can be difficult to know when to script. For coders, it can be easy to look to script before you need to, with so many opportunities to write script in ServiceNow. However, it is much better to not write script wherever possible.

If you can configure instead of scripting, it should be your first thought. This allows the tool to be used in the way it was intended and will leave you much more prepared when upgrading your instance. Not only that; one of the main reasons for using configurations over customizing is for maintenance. Configurations are easily maintained by different admins, while customization's require some basic knowledge of scripts and the logic behind them, so they tend to be harder to maintain and troubleshoot. Remember, once you start to customize, maintaining that customiszation is your responsibility.

If you find yourself unable to achieve your goals with configuration alone, then you should look to script. Even though configuration is your best option, scripting accounts for a lot of advanced functionality on most instances. Almost all mature instances will have some level of scripting done to them, but the instances that function better are the ones where scripting was performed when appropriate.

For example, if you are looking to show, hide, or make mandatory or read-only a field, then this could be done as a client script or a UI policy. If you simply needed to perform one of the actions based on a value in a field, then in this instance, a UI policy is the better choice, as it can achieve the goal without using a script. However, if you needed to perform the action based on whether the logged-in user has a particular role, then you will need to use a script. Scripting can be done in a UI policy, but I usually opt for a client script in this scenario.

 Try to avoid scripting wherever possible. Configuring an instance instead has many benefits and makes an instance easier to maintain.

Types of script

There are a multitude of different scripts you can write in ServiceNow, and the times at which they run will often dictate which is best. However, all of these scripts will fall under two categories. These are client-side scripts and server-side scripts.

These two script types will be explored further in subsequent chapters, but we will look at the basic definitions here:

- A client-side script will run in front of the user, based on the data that was delivered to the user on the web page, usually to a form or a list, in that no form submissions are required. These scripts can only use the data loaded as part of the web page to run their scripts with (if they only run on the client side), as that is the only data available. The most common client-side script is simply named a client script in ServiceNow. Some common uses for these scripts would be to draw attention to a field to change or validate a field's value.
- A server-side script will run behind the scenes once a form is submitted or a different trigger occurs. As this type of script is run on the server, it can use all the data held in the ServiceNow database, rather than just what was loaded on the web page. The business rule is the most commonly used server-side script. A business rule has many ways of functioning, but will usually run after a form submission, with common tasks to amend field values or update parent or child records.

The following table shows the most common types of scripts and whether they run on the client or server side:

Client side	Server side
Client Scripts	Business Rules
UI Policies	Access Controls
UI Actions	Script Includes
	UI Actions
	Scheduled Jobs
	Background Scripts
	Workflow Scripts
	Script Actions

You may notice from the preceding table that UI Actions appear in both the client and server side. This is because they can be run as either, and therefore, they fit into both categories. We'll discuss this and the other common script types more in later chapters.

All of the script types in the preceding table will be looked at in further detail later on, and each has an important role to play in making the most of your ServiceNow instance.

Server-side scripts are considered preferable where possible, as they can run in the background away from the user, whereas client-side scripts run in front of the user and often cause the most delay in loading pages.

It is possible for client-side scripts to call server-side scripts. This will usually result in a slight delay as the information is gathered from the database. This type of server call from a client script is best avoided where possible, but often, it is necessary. Later on, we'll discuss how to best call a server-side script from the client without creating long delays for the user.

Client- and server-side scripts are a huge part of ServiceNow scripting, and the ways you can manipulate both to your advantage will determine your overall success in scripting in ServiceNow.

When writing a new script, ask yourself whether the result needs to be shown immediately in front of the user. If not, consider a server-side script rather than a client-side script.

Script execution

The order that a script executes in ServiceNow can be extremely important. Subsequent running scripts can undo or alter the changes a previous script has made.

Some scripts can be ordered by administrators, while others cannot. It is important to know how ordering your script will affect the outcome of the script. For a script that cannot be ordered it will need to run in any order compared with other baseline or custom scripts and still function correctly.

When scripts can be ordered, they are run based on the order number assigned to them. Scripts are run in ascending order, so a script of order 50 would run before a script of order 100. Each number is not unique, though, so you are able to have multiple scripts run at order 100, which is the default for a new script. In this scenario, with scripts with the same order number, you cannot be certain which order they will run in.

Consider a scenario where script A is already in existence. Let's say that script A sets a user's active field to true. As an administrator, I write script B to set a user's active field to false. If script B has a lower order than script A, it will have no effect. This can easily be misinterpreted as script B not working correctly, but it is just being overwritten by script A. If script B is at a higher order than script A, then script B will look to be working correctly. However, script A is then redundant.

It isn't often that two scripts fly so obviously in the face of each other, but hidden among other code and multiple scripts, the above scenario is quite common in a more complicated guise. Ordering is therefore very important and quite a common reason for problems with scripts. To ensure you do not have issues with ordering in scripts, ensure you are aware of other scripts running on the field or fields you are working with before making changes with your own script.

As stated earlier, sometimes, you cannot order scripts. An example of this is for client scripts. These will essentially run in a random order, and therefore, when writing them, an administrator will need to take this into account. This means you cannot write a client script that relies on values or fields from another client script, otherwise it may break (if execution is not in the order you had hoped).

Most server-side code can be ordered, however. The order in which server-side scripts are run can be seen in the following diagram:

1. Before Business Rules with an order less than 1000

2. Before Engines (Workflows, Approvals etc.)

3. Before Business Rules with an order greater than or equal to 1000

4. Database Operation (insert, update, delete)

5. After Business Rules with an order less than 1000

6. After Engines (Workflows, Approvals etc.)

7. E-mail notifications

8. After Business Rules with an order greater than or equal to 1000

Figure 1.2: Execution order of scripts

As you can see in the preceding figure, there are a number of different times at which scripts are run, and therefore, it is important for an administrator to determine the right order for their script.

There are two significant points to note from this ordering system. The first is that, barring email notifications, a script can be called before or after the database operation. Selecting the right script execution timing can help streamline an instance. Selecting the wrong execution time will usually not cause a problem, but can be rather inefficient. Generally, it is a best practice to call a script before the database operation if the script will change values about the current record; otherwise, the script can be run after the database operation.

The second significant point is that order 1000 is an important number in ServiceNow. When I first started using ServiceNow, I wondered why so many scripts were ordered with such a high number. The reason is to run scripts in front of or behind engines. These engines include SLA, approval, and workflow engines. The main reason I have come across in my experience is to order scripts in relation to workflow scripts.

Script execution order bugs can be difficult to diagnose, as it can take a long time finding what other scripts are interfering with the current script you are working on. That is why it is important to label all code clearly and write meaningful comments within your scripts.

Introduction to scripting

ServiceNow uses JavaScript as a language for the majority of the scripts you can write or edit. If you already have a background in JavaScript, then you will certainly have a head start when it comes to writing your first scripts. The JavaScript engine used for writing scripts is updated as new versions of ServiceNow are released. The other language used is called Jelly. Not many people outside of the ServiceNow space are aware of Jelly, and it certainly wasn't a language I was familiar with before working with ServiceNow. Fortunately, Jelly is not used in the majority of scripts, and we'll cover how and where to use it in a later chapter.

Before you start writing your first script, it is important to check whether your goal can be achieved without using script. This should always be a consideration before you get started. By leveraging configurations in the form of UI policies, for example, it is possible to avoid customization all together.

When scripting, it is important to think about what you want to achieve, and which records and what fields in the database you will need access to. The most common scripts will simply need information from the current record being displayed or updated, but more complex scripts may need to access data from several different tables. It is a good practice to ensure that the database and table structure will allow you to get all the data you need for your script from the current record before you start.

One other point to note when scripting is to make sure your code is well documented, including good comments and descriptions of what goals are to be achieved. While you are writing code, it can seem that what it does will be obvious, but coming back to the same code after some time, that often will not be the case. Maintaining ServiceNow instances is a big part of an administrator's job, and trying to do this with no comments in scripts can be a laborious task. I have come across many instances with insufficient comments and descriptions, and a lot of time is initially wasted on discovering how it all hangs together. Documenting your code will not only help you over time, but will also help any other administrators who need to maintain your scripts and instances.

For example, it is important to explain what each function does:

```
/*This function returns true or false based on the whether the input
variable is 0
Inputs: input - integer
*/
function myFunction(input) {
if (input == 0) {
  return true;
} else {
  return false;
}
}
```

Most scripts will use the glide classes provided by ServiceNow, which we will discuss in the next chapter.

Script editor

When you encounter a script field in ServiceNow, it will have some additional features that allow you to create your scripts with greater ease than you would in a simple text field. This type of field is named a script type and is found throughout ServiceNow.

We will now look at this field type in detail so you can use this field to its best and understand the capabilities it has. First, let's take a look at this field in *Figure 1.2*:

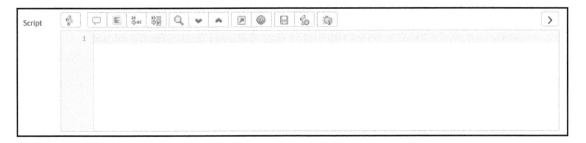

Figure 1.3: Script type field

There are a number of buttons above the field that you can use to your advantage. Let's take a look at these buttons in order, as each can assist with the code we write:

- **Scroll**: The scroll allows us to switch the syntax highlighting and script formatting on and off. It is on by default, which most will find the better option. However, if you would rather disable this and prefer writing in a simple text field, toggle this button to off. If toggled off, all the other buttons disappear to leave only a button which allows you to go to a specific line of code. Left on, this allows the script in the script field to be color coded, formatted with spacing to make it easier to read, and with syntax errors shown. The syntax errors will appear in the margin on the left, and you can hover over them to see the issue.
- **Speech bubble**: The speech bubble toggles whether the current line of script you are on is commented or not. A lot of developers will simply edit the script field itself, but it can be useful for multiple lines.
- **Aligned text**: This button formats the code in the script field. It will indent script in if statements and loops and makes the code a lot easier to read. This is a button I find very useful.
- **Replaced letters**: This button allows you to replace words or phrases in the script with different text. This is done for each instance of the word or phrase that you find, so you can replace many or a few of the words or phrases.
- **Replaced letters with text**: This icon is similar to the replace button, but it will replace all instances of a word or phrase without individually notifying you of each instance. For this reason, make sure you want to replace every specific word or phrase in the script field before using this icon.
- **Magnifying glass**: By clicking this button, we can search the text in the script field for a word or phrase.

- **Down arrow**: After performing a search, this allows the user to see the next instance of the searched for word or phrase.
- **Up arrow**: Once a search has been performed, this shows the previous word or phrase searched for in the script field.
- **Boxed arrow**: This toggles the script field between full screen and being a smaller box on the screen. This can be helpful when working on bigger scripts, to save from doing excessive scrolling.
- **Question mark**: Clicking this button shows a pop-up summary of the script editor and the shortcuts you can use.
- **Disk**: This saves the record, and the script, too.
- **Ticked scroll**: This toggles the syntax checking on and off. You will notice the left margin change size when this happens. Normally, the syntax checking is useful, but this does give the option to hide it if some of the syntax advice is not for you.
- **Bug with scroll**: By selecting this icon, the script debugger will open in a new window.

Some developers will have their own external scripting tools that they use to create the script and then paste it into script fields once complete. If doing this, ensure you have the latest version of the code in your external tool so that you do not overwrite updates from others by mistake.

This gives an overview of this type of field, and it makes scripting much easier. The syntax checking and code formatting are especially helpful tools.

Summary

In this chapter, we looked at the configuration and customization of a ServiceNow instance, and when it is appropriate to use both. We also introduced the two script types: client- and server-side scripts. This chapter also explained the running order of scripts in ServiceNow, the importance of order 1000, and how this can affect script outcomes. We introduced preparing to script, with some considerations before starting; finally, we looked at the script editor.

In the next chapter, we will look at the ServiceNow glide class. This will show you the script ServiceNow provides you, which can be used to complement your JavaScript. The glide class is a frequently used aspect of ServiceNow scripting, and understanding its use will allow you to write helpful basic scripts and serve as a great first step into writing more advanced code.

2

Exploring the ServiceNow Glide Class

In this chapter, we will explore the the ServiceNow Glide class. We will look at the exposed JavaScript APIs that allow developers to conveniently and rapidly write ServiceNow scripts. We will then look at the different classes on the server and client sides before looking at some examples of some of the most commonly used classes.

This chapter will cover the following topics:

- How to use ServiceNow exposed JavaScript APIs, including GlideRecord
- Client-side Glide classes
- Server-side Glide classes
- Examples covering some commonly used Glide classes

Using ServiceNow exposed JavaScript APIs

ServiceNow provides developers with some exposed JavaScript APIs to aid them with the scripts they write. This saves a lot of time in accessing records and fields in scripts in ServiceNow. There are a number of different classes and objects available to developers, some of which very helpful and others rarely used.

GlideRecord

One of the most common JavaScript APIs is the `GlideRecord` class, which is extremely handy and will fast become a staple of most scripting. `GlideRecord` is a way of finding and counting records in ServiceNow based on many different queries. It is quite similar to a SQL statement if that is something you are familiar with.

Let's have a look at how to use `GlideRecord`.

We'll take a look at how to query all the records in a particular table. The format of the `GlideRecord` script for this is shown in the following, with `table_name` being the only parameter. This needs to be the table name rather than the table label:

```
new GlideRecord('<table_name>');
```

We will set a variable to hold the `GlideRecord` object and define the table that will be used to query. In this example, we will use the incident table:

```
var glideRecord = new GlideRecord('incident');
```

The `glideRecord` variable now holds a `GlideRecord` object for the incident table. We then query the table and add any filtering. In this case, we will add no filter and simply return all records for the incident table, therefore showing the full script:

```
var glideRecord = new GlideRecord('incident');
glideRecord.query();
while (glideRecord.next()) {
    //Code in this loop will be run against all incident records
}
```

This is a very important part of ServiceNow scripting as it is the way coders can access the records in ServiceNow by cycling through them and applying some code to each relevant record.

Now that we've seen how to set up a `GlideRecord` query, let's have a look at the script line that can filter a `GlideRecord` for us:

```
variable.addQuery('<field_name>', '<operator>',
'<value_to_compare_against_field>')
```

Here, we filter based on a field name and compare the value in that field using the operator to the value we define. The default `operator` is that the value equals the value in the field so if this is the operator we need, we can just leave it out.

Let's have a look at another example. This time, we'll look to query all the problem records with a critical priority using our filter line:

```
var glideRecord = new GlideRecord('problem');
glideRecord.addQuery('priority', 1);
glideRecord.query();
while (glideRecord.next()) {
    //Code in this loop will be run against all problem records with a
priority of critical.
}
```

As you can see in the preceding code, we omitted the operator because we want problem records with a priority equal to 1 and therefore we did not need to include it.

In the examples so far, we have cycled through all of the records, but we can amend the loop to return just one if it exists by changing the `while` to an `if`. This is often helpful when checking whether all tasks of a parent record are complete. Let's look at how it would change our script from our last example:

```
var glideRecord = new GlideRecord('problem');
glideRecord.addQuery('priority', 1);
glideRecord.query();
if (glideRecord.next()) {
    //Code in this loop will be run against one problem record with a
priority of 1 if one exists.
}
```

This code could be used to check whether any priority critical problems exist and will run some code against it if one does.

You can add more than one query and each record that is returned will need to satisfy each filter being defined. In that respect, it is quite like searching for a house. You could just search for all houses, but you more likely would want to build filters up to find exactly what you are looking for – price range, bedrooms, location, and so on.

With all of these filters adding up and essentially creating a series of logical AND statements, we also need a way of creating a logical OR statement. In the same way you can add a query line, you can also add an OR condition line of script. Let's see how it works:

```
var glideRecord = new GlideRecord('change_request');
var orQuery = glideRecord.addQuery('risk', 1);
```

```
orQuery.addOrCondition('risk', 2);
glideRecord.query();
while (glideRecord.next()) {
    //Code in this loop will be run against all change request records that
are a very high or high risk.
}
```

As you can see, the original condition is stored in a variable, orQuery, and then the OR condition is added to this variable before the query takes place. This type of query is handy if you want certain code to execute when a record is in a certain set of states.

There are many ways to achieve the same goal in ServiceNow and to show this, we can set up the same filter on change records using a different operator. This uses the fact that many values of choice lists in ServiceNow are numbers so we can just search for all change requests with a risk of greater than or equal to 2:

```
var glideRecord = new GlideRecord('change_request');
glideRecord.addQuery('risk', '>=', 2);
glideRecord.query();
while (glideRecord.next()) {
    //Code in this loop will be run against all change request records that
are a very high or high risk.
}
```

This second example would usually be considered better than the first, as it is using fewer lines of code.

Now we have looked at how to get the records we want, we will look at how to alter the records we have found. First, we'll take a look at a simple update to a record. In this example, we will update all incident records with a high urgency and move it down to medium:

```
var glideRecord = new GlideRecord('incident');
glideRecord.addQuery('urgency', 1);
glideRecord.query();
while (glideRecord.next()) {
    //Change all high urgency incidents to medium urgency
    glideRecord.urgency = 2;
    glideRecord.update();
}
```

When updating a record, you can amend many of the fields and then use update to save the changes. This is a very important method and is relatively simple to use.

The final examples we will look at are how to delete records. Obviously, be careful when deleting records and ensure the query you have written is correct before executing.

There are two main methods of deleting records: either individually through looping or all in one go. Let's look at deleting individual records first. In this example, we'll delete all of the `network` category incidents:

```
var glideRecord = new GlideRecord('incident');
glideRecord.addQuery('category', 'network');
glideRecord.query();
while (glideRecord.next()) {
    glideRecord.deleteRecord();
}
```

Next, we'll look at how to delete all of the queried records in one go:

```
var glideRecord = new GlideRecord('incident');
glideRecord.addQuery('category', 'network');
glideRecord.deleteMultiple();
```

As you can see, the script for both of these `delete` methods is quite different, but the end result is the same. The `deleteMultiple` method is a quicker, more efficient method; however, it will delete everything in one go. If there is a large amount of data to be deleted, this can cause resources to be tied up for a long time. I have used the `deleteRecord` method instead in the case of a large volume of data to stagger the deletion of records in smaller groups of records.

> When creating a `delete` script, try executing it first with the `delete` method commented out and some logging to show what you have deleted. If the logging brings back the records you want, then go ahead with the deletion. This helps to ensure the wrong records are not removed.

That concludes `GlideRecord` for now, but it will feature again throughout the book, further proving how important it is.

Server-side Glide classes

Now we will look at some of the server-side classes that we can use for our scripts. Remember these methods will not work on the client side so make sure you are aware whether the script you are writing is on the server side.

GlideSystem

`GlideSystem` is probably the most commonly used server-side classes. Let's have a look at how we can utilize this class to aid us in our scripting.

ServiceNow shortens `GlideSystem` to `gs` in scripts so the methods of `GlideSystem` will be prefixed with `gs`.

Let's start by seeing how to get a user's `sys_id` using `GlideSystem`:

```
var userID = gs.getUserID();
```

This puts the logged-in user's `sys_id` in the `userID` variable. This can be helpful as you can use this in scripts where you may want to execute different lines of script depending on the attributes of the user. Now we have the user's `sys_id`, we could use a `GlideRecord` query to return the fields we desire. ServiceNow does allow us to obtain some of this information in an easier way.

We can get the `user` object and then use some helpful functions to access further information about the user. To get the `user` object, we simply write the following:

```
var userObject = gs.getUser();
```

Next, let us see some of the most helpful functions:

```
gs.getUser().getFullName();
gs.getUser().getEmail();
gs.getUser().getLocation();
gs.getUser().getManagerID();
gs.getUser().getCompanyID();
```

Most of the preceding code is fairly self-explanatory, but the ID functions will return the `sys_id` of the record in the same way as the user `sys_id`.

The user's details can be useful for sending notifications and setting up approvals and condition scripts based on locations or companies.

Whilst we are on user data, it is often important to find out which roles a user has to decide what they should have access to. `GlideSystem` allows us to see whether a user has a certain role in the script, as shown in the following example:

```
if (gs.hasRole('admin')) {
    //Run code for administrators only
}
```

The `hasRole` method is especially useful when using script to allow or restrict data to a user. It can also be used to hide or show UI actions that would require an elevated privilege to use. One thing to note is that the `hasRole` method will always return `true` for an administrator.

`GlideSystem` is also good for letting the user know what has happened during a script through an output message for the user. This is done using an `Info` or `Error` message. The `Info` message is displayed in a nice blue box and the `Error` message, unsurprisingly, in a red one at the top of the form once processing has completed and the next screen has loaded.

Let's have a look at how to script these:

```
gs.addInfoMessage('Record saved successfully.');
gs.addErrorMessage('Error in script.');
```

These are fairly simple lines, but are very handy in keeping a user updated with how scripts performed when processed and whether there were any problems. I tend to use the info message to let a user know an action completed successfully when it is not immediately obvious on the screen they are returned to. An `Error` message is good when something in a script goes wrong. Remember that this message will be displayed to a variety of users so it is best to not get too technical in the message.

`GlideSystem` also allows us to perform logging so that we can debug our server-side scripts. As server-side scripts are running behind the scenes, we need a way of logging what happened in the script so we can look at it later and review and debug if necessary.

The little bit of script that is the most common for this is `log`. Simply used, this is just a string of text to send to the logs:

```
gs.log('Logging Message');
```

This message will now be visible in the **Script Log Statements** module in the application navigator. If you are looking through older script in a ServiceNow instance, you will often find these log messages. Sometimes they are commented out in case they are needed again for debugging and sometimes they should have been commented out and the developer forgot.

If many logs are being created, it can be helpful to give your log a unique source so you can more easily search for only logs from your particular source. Let's have a look at what this looks like:

```
gs.log('Logging Message', 'My Script Log');
```

This message will then appear in the system log with a source of `My Script Log`. One thing to note is that it will no longer appear in the **Script Log Statements** module as you have changed the source to a custom source.

`GlideSystem` is probably the most useful server-side Glide class and there are more methods on top of the ones we have discussed.

GlideDateTime

`GlideDateTime` is, unsurprisingly, about scripting with dates and times, specifically the `GlideDateTime` object. The `GlideDateTime` object is mainly used to populate **Date/Time** fields and the methods around them to manipulate dates and times to add or remove time to a field.

First, let's look at defining a new `GlideDateTime`:

```
var glideDT = new GlideDateTime();
```

This will put the current date and time in GMT format in the `glideDT` field as part of a `GlideDateTime` object. This can be helpful if you want to compare a date in a field with the current date and time.

Now, with any date and time scripting, time zones are always an issue. One of the best ways to get around this is to use the display value to make sure dates and times are displayed to users in the correct format for the user who is viewing it. Let's look at how this is done by logging the display value:

```
var glideDT = new GlideDateTime();
gs.log(glideDT.getDisplayValue());
```

This is very helpful in scripting to ensure that all users see the correct times.

Sometimes there will also be the requirement to add or remove time from a **Date/Time** field using script. There are a few methods to add various amounts of time to or from a **Date/Time** field. We'll have a look at one of these; the others work in a very similar way:

```
var glideDT = new GlideDateTime();
glideDT.addDaysLocalTime(1);
```

In this example, we would be adding 1 day, so 24 hours, to the current day and time:

```
var glideDT = new GlideDateTime();
glideDT.addDaysLocalTime(-1);
```

By using a negative number, we actually subtract time from the object so the preceding example would actually give you the date and time of this time yesterday.

GlideDateTime is helpful when dealing with dates and times, which can often be a headache in coding. Remember, when using negative figures in addtime methods, this reduces the time instead of increasing it.

GlideElement

GlideElement provides methods for dealing with the fields in a GlideRecord object. This class is one of the smaller ones in ServiceNow.

One very handy set of methods in this class is detecting changes to a field. This is very helpful in closing down records. Sometimes we may want to run some script on closure of the record, but not every time the record is updated. This is when the changesTo method can be used. We'll assume we are using an incident, in this case where the closed state is 7:

```
if  (current.state.changesTo('7')) {
    //Run some closure script
}
```

This preceding example will allow for some script to run when the record is closed, but only when it moves to being closed. If the closed record is subsequently updated, then this script will not run again. That is why this method is so helpful. You can also use changes and changesFrom methods as part of this set.

You may or may not be aware of what current refers to at this point, but we will take a closer look at this when we look at business rules in Chapter 5, *Introduction to Server-Side Scripting*.

Another helpful set of methods in GlideElement is checking whether a user is able to create, read, or write to records. We can use this to see whether a user should be able to perform these actions, which can be very helpful in UI action conditions.

Let's see how it works:

```
if (current.canCreate()) {
    //Run some creation script for the current record type
}
```

This will check whether the logged-in user is able to create a record of the current type (incident, change request, and so on) and, if so, then run the script inside the if statement. We can also use the canRead and canWrite methods in a similar way.

With `GlideElement` being a smaller class, it is not as well used as some of the other server-side classes, but some of its methods are very helpful, particularly in UI actions.

GlideAggregate

The `GlideAggregate` class is an extension of `GlideRecord` and works in a similar way. The difference is that `GlideRecord` tends to give you database objects whereas `GlideAggregate` deals in counts and numbers.

We'll take a quick look at how `GlideAggregate` works:

```
var counter = new GlideAggregate('incident');
counter.addAggregate('COUNT');
counter.query();
if (counter.next()) {
    var noOfIncidents = counter.getAggregate('COUNT');
}
```

This first example will give us the number of incidents in the database and place it in the `noOfIncidents` field. We can add `addQuery` lines in exactly the same way we would for `GlideRecord` if we wanted to reduce the number of incident records we returned.

As well as `COUNT`, we can also use `SUM`, `MAX`, `MIN`, and `AVG` to get the total sum, maximum number, minimum number, and average, respectively.

I don't find `GlideAggregate` used that regularly, but it is an efficient way to count records.

Client-side Glide classes

The client-side Glide classes are for use in scripts that are run directly in front of the user. These include manipulating and working with form fields and user data and being able to call server-side scripts to return values in the database.

GlideForm

I would say that GlideForm or `g_form` is the most used client-side class. It is mainly used for getting data from the fields on the form and setting values to those fields as well. We can also change elements of those fields using `g_form`.

We'll start by looking at how to get and set values from and into fields:

```
var stateValue = g_form.getValue('state');
```

The string value inside the speech marks is the database name for the field. Make sure you use the name rather than the label when getting a value using g_form. The getValue method essentially puts the value of a field into a variable for you. This then allows you to use that variable to check against other data or pass as a parameter into a function:

```
g_form.setValue('state', '6');
```

The setValue method will immediately set the value of the field on the screen to what the script dictates. In this example, presuming we are on the incident table, the state field would change to resolved. Remember, here, we are using the number 6 as that is the choice value for the resolved state in ServiceNow.

It is also worth noting that the value at this point will only have changed on the screen in front of the user. The field in the database will not be updated until the record itself is.

Using g_form, we can also change elements of the field itself and not just the value it holds. Let's have a look at how to make a field mandatory, show and hide a field, and make a field read-only. The best practice for these actions is to use a UI policy; however, the conditions in a UI policy are limited so sometimes we need to use a script to perform these actions.

We'll start by setting a field to mandatory:

```
g_form.setMandatory('short_description', true);
```

This example would set the short description field to mandatory. If we want to reverse this, we just need to change true to false in the line. This can be helpful when using UI actions to move through states of a record and to ensure certain fields are filled in before moving to the next stage. This change to the mandatory state of the field is just temporary; if the form is reloaded, then the field will go back to its original mandatory or non-mandatory state.

To change whether a field is visible, we can use the following code:

```
g_form.setDisplay('assigned_to', false);
```

This example will hide the assigned to field, but we can show it again by changing false to true in the line of script. This method isn't used that often as this action can usually be performed by a UI policy. This method will allow the space the field has left behind to be reclaimed by other fields. The setVisible method is very similar to the setDisplay method except a blank space is left where the field used to be, which tends to make setDisplay the better aesthetic choice.

The method for setting a field to be read-only is as follows:

```
g_form.setReadOnly('description', true);
```

The preceding example will set the description field to read-only, meaning the field cannot be edited. This will only be while the current form is loaded and will revert back to its original state of read-only or not when the form reloads.

There are also some useful bits of information that g_form can get for you as well. To begin with, let's see how you can get the unique value or sys_id of a record using g_form:

```
var sysID = g_form.getUniqueValue();
```

The example puts the sys_id of the record in the sysID variable. This can be useful if you want the sys_id value even before the record is saved.

We can also use code to check whether the record has been saved or not yet:

```
if (g_form.isNewRecord()) {
    //Run script only for new records
}
```

This isNewRecord method allows us to write script for only new records or for only records that have already been saved. This can help you to decide whether to insert or update a record at the end of the script.

GlideUser

GlideUser or g_user is a class all about the attributes of the user. It is not the biggest class, but some of the properties and methods can be used quite frequently.

One of the most helpful of these is being able to get the user ID, the sys_id of the user, through a property. This can be very helpful to send to another script so that the script knows which user is currently logged in or for getting the user record.

Let's have a look at how to get this ID:

```
var userSys_ID = g_user.userID;
```

In the example, the userSys_ID variable will be the sys_id of the logged-in user.

TIP

When getting a user record, it is best practice to use the `sys_id` rather than a name to obtain the record. This is because there is a chance users in the database may have the same name, whereas the `sys_id` of a user will always be unique.

We can also use `g_user` to get the full name of the logged-in user. This can be helpful if we want to display a user's name in messages displayed to them or in fields.

We can get a user's full name by using the following example:

```
var name = g_user.getFullName();
alert('The logged in user is ' + name);
```

This preceding example sets the name variable to be the user's full name. Let's assume I am the logged-in user here. The `alert` method shows a pop-up message to the user, so in this scenario, it would say `The logged in user is Andrew Kindred`.

Sometimes when scripting, we want to know whether the user has a specific role so we can decide whether or not a piece of code should run for them or not. To do this on the client side, we can use the `hasRole` method. It works in a very similar way to the server-side `GlideSystem` method.

Let's look at an example of the `hasRole` method:

```
if (g_user.hasRole('itil') {
    //Run code for user with the itil role only
}
```

As you can see, this code is very similar to the server-side code. We can use an `if` statement to ensure that we only run certain code for users with a certain role.

There are a few other methods relating to basic user data and roles, but we have covered the most useful ones here.

Additional client-side Glide classes

The two classes we have looked at so far are the most useful and also the easiest to begin with. However, there are some other helpful client-side Glide classes. We will look at these other Glide classes later in the book, as they tie in nicely with some of the types of client-side script and specific actions you may want to achieve with your code.

Script examples

Now we've looked at some server- and client-side Glide classes, we can take a look at some examples of using these methods and properties in some slightly more complex blocks of code to achieve our goals in ServiceNow.

Let's start by having a look at some GlideRecord examples.

This time, we'll use GlideRecord multiple times, one inside another. This is a technique you will no doubt use quite often as you progress with your scripting. It has certainly served me well over the years.

In this example, we'll take a look at creating a problem record for every critical priority incident:

```
var incRec = new GlideRecord('incident');
incRec.addQuery('priority', 1);
incRec.query();
while (incRec.next()) {

    //Critical incident found, create a new problem record
    var newProblemRec = new GlideRecord('problem');
    newProblemRec.cmdb_ci = incRec.cmdb_ci;
    newProblemRec.short_description = incRec.short_description;
    var newInsertedRecord = newProblemRec.insert();

    //Update the incident with the problem reference
    incRec.problem_id = newInsertedRecord;
    incRec.update();
}
```

In the preceding example, we've found all critical incidents using a GlideRecord query. Once we find a matching incident record, we create a new problem record using insert, copying the configuration item and short description fields from the incident over to the problem record also. Once the problem record has been inserted, we store its unique value in the newInsertedRecord variable so that we can add that value into the incident record-related problem field. This ensures the two records are linked and that the incident will appear in the related list on the problem record.

We can see what this script would look like in a scheduled job in the following screenshot:

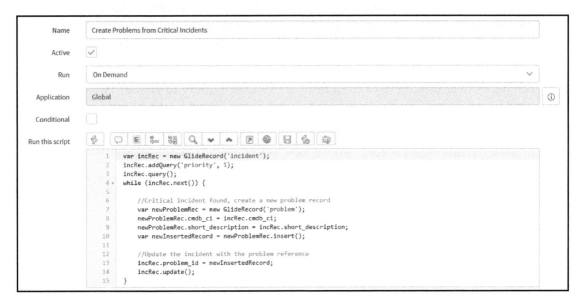

Figure 2.1: Scheduled job for creating problems from critical incidents

We will take an in-depth look at scheduled jobs in `Chapter 6`, *Advanced Server-Side Scripting*. This figure gives you an idea of seeing the layout of Glide classes in a ServiceNow script field.

Using a `GlideRecord` inside a `GlideRecord` is incredibly useful, as we can create, update, or search within a `GlideRecord` query `while` loop.

If we know the `sys_id` of a record, there is a shortcut called `get` we can use to obtain the record directly. We can use our user-based methods to show a quick way of getting the user record.

The following script uses this `get` method to quickly access the user record we require:

```
var userRec = new GlideRecord('sys_user');
userRec.get(gs.getUserID());
userRec.title = 'Manager';
userRec.update();
```

Using the `get` method, we have quickly retrieved the currently logged-in user's user record, also using our `GlideSystem` method to get the user ID. We could also put a `sys_id` contained in quotes here for the `get` method parameter. The example then sets the title of the user to be a manager and saves the record. Running this code will make any logged-in user have a manager as their title.

This technique saves us having to use a full `GlideRecord` query to get the user record that we need. This means not having to search through the user table, which saves resources and also extra lines of code.

We can see what this example code would look like in a business rule in ServiceNow:

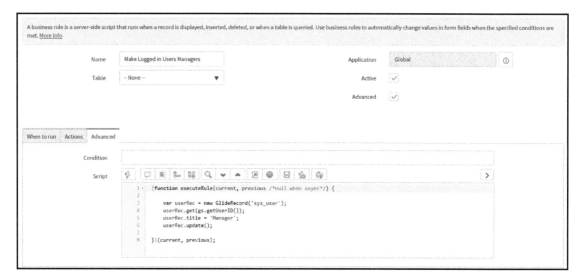

Figure 2.2: Business rule making logged-in users managers

We will take an in-depth look at business rules in `Chapter 5`, *Introduction to Server-Side Scripting*. They are often used for server-side scripting. We would also need to add a value to the table field so that our business rule knows which table to run this script against.

We can also use some of the techniques we've learned in this chapter to send specific messages to users. Let's assume we want to give users a different message depending on what roles they have:

```
if (gs.hasRole('admin')) {
    gs.addErrorMessage('Error with solaris server');
} else if (gs.hasRole('itil')) {
    gs.addErrorMessage('Server error');
} else {
    gs.addErrorMessage('An error has occurred, please contact your
administrator');
}
```

This server-side example will display an error message to a user based on what roles they have. This can be useful to display additional information to users who will understand it and it will keep the details simple for users who do not have as much technical expertise.

This code adds error messages that are displayed to the user when the form loads at the top of the screen. By using the `if` statements, we will only ever display one message to the user and, in our example, the most suitable one for the role of that user.

We can also set some values on a form based on whether it is a new form or not. Perhaps we want to make all new incident forms have an inquiry/help category, but not change any incidents that already exist.

We can see the script we would need for this as follows:

```
if (g_form.isNewRecord()) {
    g_form.setValue('category', 'inquiry');
}
```

With this client-side script example, we would only set the category field to `inquiry/help` if it was a new record. Remember that this would only set the field on the screen on the client side and would not save the field as this value until the record was saved.

This type of code can be very useful for setting up records in a certain way whilst they are being created. Sometimes it can be that fields are not shown on creation of a new record and are only viewed once the record has been created.

We can see this code in a client script in the following screenshot:

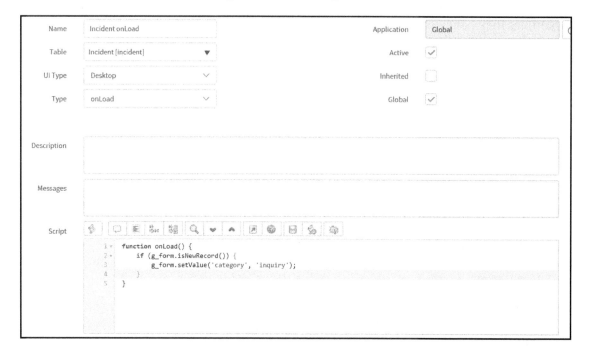

Figure 2.3: Client script setting the incident category

We will look at client scripts further in the next chapter and they are usually the main source of client-side scripting in an instance.

If we wanted to only run script when the record is not new, we can simply place a exclamation mark in front of the `if` condition to negate the expression and give us the option to add code for updating existing records.

The `if` statement would instead look like this:

```
if (!g_form.isNewRecord()) {
}
```

As you can see, we can use many of the methods we saw earlier in the chapter together to achieve the scripting goals we are looking for.

Summary

In this chapter, we looked at using exposed JavaScript APIs and the well-used `GlideRecord` class. We also looked at server-side and client-side Glide classes and the properties and methods of each that can be used to enhance your scripting. Finally, we looked at some more complex examples of scripting, combining these properties and methods to show what can be achieved and how the properties and methods can be used together.

In the next chapter, we will explore the basics of client-side scripting. We will look at client scripts, UI policies, when to use these scripts, and how to test them. Plus we'll add some helpful examples to show some great ways to get the most out of client-side scripting.

3
Introduction to Client-Side Scripting

In this chapter, we will start taking a look at client-side basics. This will give you an idea of where and how to write your client-side scripts and how to test them. We'll also take a look at a few examples for getting started in this area.

In this chapter, we will be looking at these topics:

- Client scripts
- UI policies
- How and when to write client-side scripts
- Testing a client-side script
- Basic client-side script examples

Client scripts

Client scripts are generally the client-side scripts most used by developers. By default, a client script will run on all views of a form, but it can be set up to only run for a certain view by unchecking the global checkbox and entering a specific view into the view field that appears. Client scripts can also be inherited to tables that extend from a different table. For example, a client script on the task table can be inherited to tables that extend it, like the incident, change, and problem tables. To allow tables to inherit a client script, the inherit checkbox must be set.

The script in a client script can be run at different times, depending on when the developer chooses. This choice is made by selecting a type for the client script.

There are four types of client script, and these are:

- onLoad
- onChange
- onSubmit
- onCellEdit

Let's take a look at each type and when you may want to use each to achieve your scripting goals.

onLoad

The onLoad client script type runs script when a form is loaded. This can be helpful to manipulate data on a form before a user starts using it. Sometimes, when a form loads slowly, it is possible to see onLoad client scripts doing their job.

When selecting the onLoad type, the script field will be populated with the onLoad function ServiceNow provides for you, as long as the script field hasn't already been edited. The script looks as follows:

```
function onLoad() {
    //Type appropriate comment here, and begin script below

}
```

This is the onLoad function to put your script into. Any script running onLoad will take time to run and slow down loading time, so it is always worth trying to keep onLoad client scripts to a minimum, and short, if necessary. I have been involved in projects simply to reduce the amount of onLoad client scripts on forms to reduce load times.

Try to have only one onLoad client script for each table, rather than multiple. This makes it easy to maintain, as all onLoad code is in one place, and you can be completely confident of the order the onLoad code will run in.

In the following figure, *Figure 3.1*, we can see what this type of client script will look like:

Name	Incident onLoad			Application	Global	
Table	Incident [incident]	▼		Active	✓	
UI Type	Desktop	⌄		Inherited	☐	
Type	onLoad	⌄		Global	✓	

Description

Messages

Script

```
1  function onLoad() {
2      //Type appropriate comment here, and begin script below
3
4  }
```

Figure 3.1: Sample onLoad client script

In the preceding figure, we can see an onLoad client script ready to be written for the incident table. As the comment states in the code, replace the comment in the code with the functionality of your script, and then begin writing underneath the comment inside the onLoad function.

onChange

The onChange client script runs when a selected field is changed on the form. It is important to note that an onChange script will also run when the form is loaded. This type of script is often used to auto-populate other fields on a form, based on data in the field the onChange script is running on. For example, if a user is selected on a form, other user data on the form, like company and job title, could be populated using an onChange script.

In the same way that ServiceNow provides a script function in `onLoad` scripts, an `onChange` function is also provided. This is slightly more complicated, so let's take a look:

```
function onChange(control, oldValue, newValue, isLoading, isTemplate) {
    if (isLoading || newValue === '') {
        return;
    }

    //Type appropriate comment here, and begin script below

}
```

The `onChange` function gives us five parameters that we can use inside the function in our script. Here is what each of these parameters gives us:

- `control`: The dynamic HTML of the field that has changed
- `oldValue`: The value in the changed field when the form was loaded
- `newValue`: The new value that has been entered into the changed field
- `isLoading`: Is true if the form is loading; otherwise, false
- `isTemplate`: Is true if the change has occurred as part of a template load; otherwise, false

You can also see that a little scripting has already been done by ServiceNow. This `if` statement checks if the form is loading or if the new value of the changed field is empty. If either of these cases is true, the script returns from the function, essentially canceling the script. In most cases, this is quite helpful, but it is good to understand this `if` statement, as sometimes you will want to amend it if you want code to run during loading or on the field changing to an empty value.

For example, if you have cleared a user field where additional user data has been added to the form, you will also want to clear the additional user data. In this instance, you will want to remove the condition where the code returns from the function if the `newValue` parameter is blank.

When selecting the `onChange` type, the option to pick a field for the script to run against will be visible to the developer. The fields available in this field are dependent on the value in the table field.

We can see an onChange type client script in *Figure 3.2*:

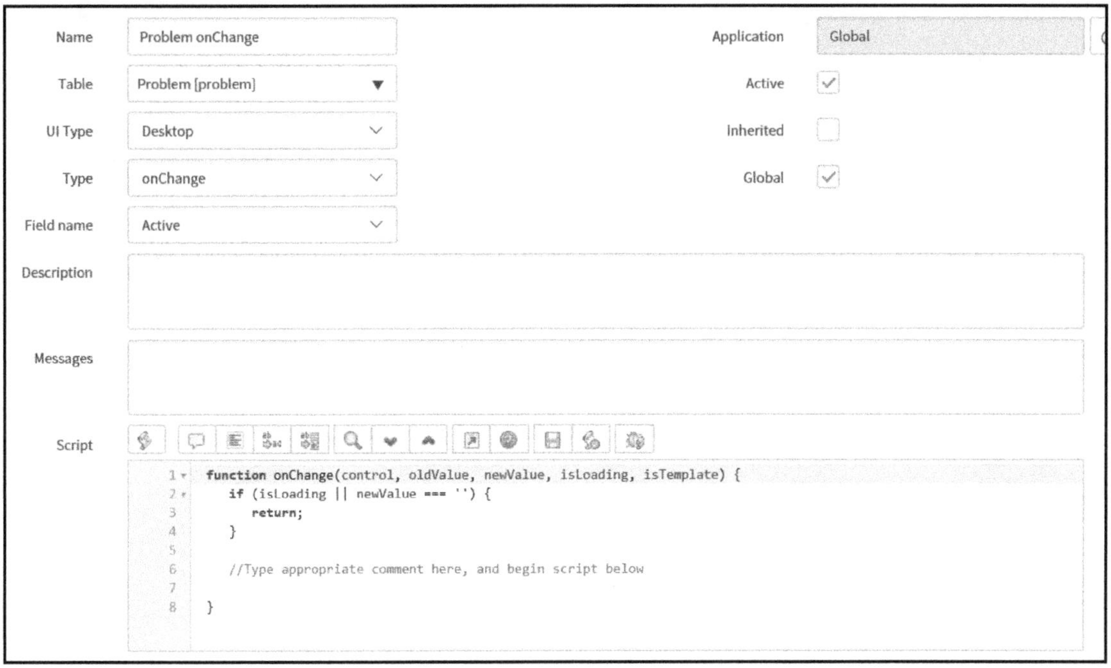

Name	Problem onChange		Application	Global
Table	Problem [problem] ▼		Active	✓
UI Type	Desktop ⌄		Inherited	☐
Type	onChange ⌄		Global	✓
Field name	Active ⌄			
Description				
Messages				

```
1  function onChange(control, oldValue, newValue, isLoading, isTemplate) {
2      if (isLoading || newValue === '') {
3          return;
4      }
5
6      //Type appropriate comment here, and begin script below
7
8  }
```

Figure 3.2: Sample onChange client script

In the preceding figure, we can see an onChange client script for the problem table. Pay particular attention to the **Field name** field, which defaults to **Active**, as that is the field that needs to change for this script to run. It can be easy to forget to change this field and wonder why your script is not executing when you are expecting it to.

onSubmit

The onSubmit client script type runs when a form is saved. This type of script is not that widely used, as we can often use server-side script to perform actions for us once a record is saved, but it can be helpful, as it provides a final chance to execute client-side script before server-side script is run.

The script ServiceNow provides for `onSubmit` is quite similar to `onLoad`:

```
function onSubmit() {
    //Type appropriate comment here, and begin script below

}
```

The `onSubmit` script type can be used to check field values before a save takes place and abort the save if invalid values exist in fields.

When considering writing an `onSubmit` script, it is worth thinking about whether that script could run on the server side instead. This is because the client script runs in front of the user, and further processing must wait until the script finishes, whereas on the server side, the code is executed away from the user and can be executed alongside other scripts.

If you want to abort the form being submitted, return false from the `onSubmit` function.

We can see an `onSubmit` example in *Figure 3.3*:

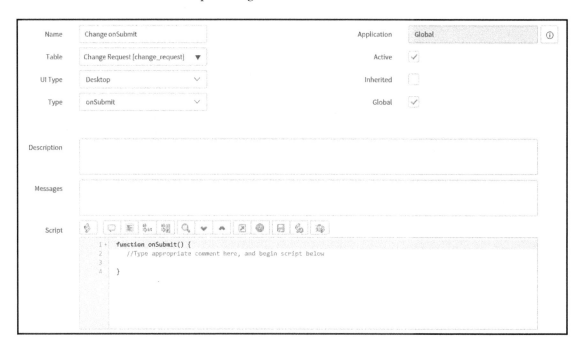

Figure 3.3: Sample onSubmit client script

For our `onSubmit` client script example, we can see that this client script is ready for the script to be added for the change table.

onCellEdit

The `onCellEdit` type of client script runs when a cell is edited on the list view of a table. This is the only client script type that does not run on the form view of a table. This type of client script is helpful to ensure that the rules you want to stick to are also enforced on list views of a table.

The script that ServiceNow provides for `onCellEdit` scripts looks a little different from the other client script types:

```
function onCellEdit(sysIDs, table, oldValues, newValue, callback) {
   var saveAndClose = true;
  //Type appropriate comment here, and begin script below

  callback(saveAndClose);
}
```

It is worth noting that these scripts could be for multiple records, as you can edit more than one using a list. As you can see, there are quite a few different parameters in this slightly different type of script. We'll have a look at what each one of those parameters gives us:

- `sysIDs`: All of the `sys_id` unique IDs of the records being edited in an array.
- `table`: The current table of the records being edited.
- `oldValues`: The old values of all the cells being edited.
- `newValue`: The new value to be put into all the cells being edited.
- `callback`: A callback that allows the execution of further `onCellEdit` scripts or commits the change made if no further scripts exist. A `true` or `false` parameter can be passed, which will either allow further scripts and commit changes, or stop execution of further scripts and not commit the change, respectively.

These scripts tend to not be used that frequently, as server-side scripts like business rules can often be used to perform the functionality needed. Editing records in the list can also be a powerful tool for updating multiple records at once, so this is sometimes locked down to only certain users to prevent less knowledgeable users from causing issues.

An `onCellEdit` client script example can be viewed in *Figure 3.4*:

Figure 3.4: Sample onCellEdit client script

The client script in the preceding figure is an `onCellEdit` for the requested item table. Again, for this type of script, ensure the **Field name** field is set to the value you require, as the script will only run on a change to this field in the list view.

UI policies

UI policies are a more configurable version of client scripts. An administrator sets a condition and then uses actions or scripts to amend fields. Using configuration, a developer can change whether a field is mandatory, visible, and read-only. If these are the changes you are considering making to a field, a UI policy is usually the best option. UI policies are easier to understand and maintain for other administrators than client scripts.

UI policies can also be scripted based on the condition set, as in, you can run code if the condition matches and you can run code if the condition does not match. Setting the condition in a UI policy is much like setting a condition elsewhere in ServiceNow, as it uses the standard condition builder.

UI policies run against a table, but because you can use the condition builder, a number of fields can be used as part of the condition built. UI policies come with some tick boxes that dictate when the UI policy should be applied. In the following, we'll take a look at the different choices and how they change when a policy is applied:

- `Global`: Set by default, this means the UI policy will run on all views by default, although by unticking the global tick box, you can select a specific view.
- `On load`: Set by default, too, this tick box, when checked, runs the policy when the form is loaded, as well as when fields are changed.
- `Reverse if false`: If the condition is not true, then reverse the effects of the UI policy. This is set by default.
- `Inherit`: Unset by default, this allows tables that extend the selected table to inherit the policy. For example, a policy on the task table would be inherited by the incident table if this was set.

A UI policy has UI policy actions associated to it that will take effect when the condition matches, or in reverse if the reverse if false checkbox is set. These actions allow for fields to be made mandatory, visible, read-only, or a combination of these effects. UI policy actions are considered as configurations, and considered best practice when taking these actions on fields.

If you want to achieve more with a UI policy, there are options to script on matching or not matching the given condition. This is rarely used, as client scripts tend to fit this requirement better, but let's look at how it works.

Firstly, to script in a UI policy, you must set the **Run scripts** checkbox. This makes two fields appear: **Execute if true** and **Execute if false**. These are fairly self explanatory in that they will run if the condition defined in the UI policy matches true or false.

ServiceNow gives us the function to put our code into, which looks as follows:

```
function onCondition() {

}
```

This function is the same in both the **Execute if true** or **Execute if false** script fields.

UI policies are very useful for making fields mandatory, visible, and read-only. The ability to configure rather than customize is certainly considered best practice if thinking of scripting in UI policies, though it is often best to use a client script. This is because you only have to maintain one script with a client script, rather than the two on a UI policy. It is also easier to code for all eventualities in client scripts, rather than just matching or not matching a set condition, as in UI policies.

We can see a UI policy in *Figure 3.5* showing the script form section:

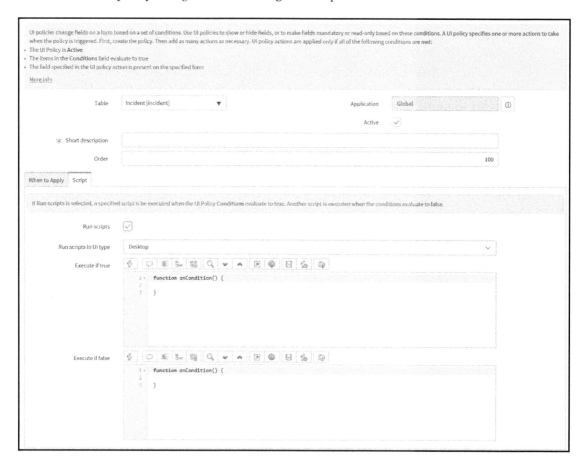

Figure 3.5: Sample UI policy showing script fields

In the preceding figure, we can see a UI policy currently set to run on the incident table. It is important, if we use the two script fields we can see, that we cover the scenarios of the condition of the UI policy being true and false with these two scripts.

How and when to write client-side scripts

Client-side scripts should be written when a developer wants to change the screen in front of the user. This could be a change to a field value, visibility, or another change. Every time client-side scripts are run, it requires resources from the instance, and so keeping client-side scripting to a minimum is important.

If you can make a change on the server side rather than the client side, then is it considered best practice to do so. This will then keep loading times shorter and improve the user experience.

Let's have a look at some common uses for client-side scripting and how best to achieve these tasks.

Making fields mandatory, visible, or read-only

For making fields mandatory, visible, or read-only, it is best to use a UI policy. This method uses configuration rather than customization, and is easier to maintain.

Scripting does not need to be done in this case, as you can use UI policy actions to achieve your goal. ServiceNow makes these actions easy to set up with the condition builder.

Populating fields based on the value of another field

Another popular use for client-side scripting is populating a field based on the value of another. A common use of this is when selecting a user in a field and then wanting, for example, to automatically populate the company, telephone number, and job title.

For this example, you will want to use an `onChange` client script. By setting the `onChange` field to be the user field, you can then get the rest of the user data using a client script. The best practice for this is to use a `GlideAjax` call, which we will explore in advanced client scripting later in the next chapter.

Showing/hiding form sections

Sometimes you will want to show only certain form sections to different types of users. This can be based on a number of variables, but often it will be based on the roles a user has or the groups they belong to.

For this requirement, an `onLoad` client script can be used. This will ensure that before the form is available to the user, the required form sections can be hidden.

Review

We have looked at some of the more common uses of client scripting, but this is by no means an exhaustive list. When considering writing scripts on the client side, it is often worth thinking about how necessary they are and if they can be better placed in server-side script. Remember that client-side scripts increase load times, so try to keep them to a minimum.

Testing client-side scripts

Testing scripts in ServiceNow can be done in a few ways. Fortunately, client-side scripts can be some of the easiest to test, because the script is running in front of the user, and therefore, logging and feedback on scripts can be shown directly to the user, too.

Alert

One of the simplest ways to debug client script is to use the alert functionality. `alert` simply pops up a message window displaying information you choose to include. This can be useful for showing the values of fields or variables at certain times, or simply to confirm that certain functions were entered.

Let's see how `alert` works in the following code:

```
alert('Debug Message');
```

The preceding script will simply show a pop-up message to the user saying `Debug Message`. It is a simple line of code to write and provides instant feedback.

Let's have a look at how we can use `alert` to help us test our code:

```
function onLoad() {
alert('Start of script');
var shortDescBefore = g_form.getValue('short_description');
alert('The short description beforehand is ' + shortDescBefore);
g_form.setValue('short_description', 'Alerting Issue');
var shortDescAfter = g_form.getValue('short_description');
alert('The short description afterwards is ' + shortDescAfter);

}
```

In the preceding example, we are using three messages to test that the script is working how we would like it to. The first will simply alert us to the script starting by showing the user **Start of script**. This can be helpful to check that JavaScript is running correctly on a browser or that other client scripts are not causing an error that stops this script from running.

The second message gives us the value of the short description as the form is loading. We are storing the value of the short description in the `shortDescBefore` variable and using it in our alert. We can combine strings of text and variables together in an alert by using the plus sign between them.

The third message shows the value of the short description field after we have used the `g_form setValue` method to amend it. The third message will read **The short description afterwards is Alerting Issue**.

Using `alert` allows us to test and also debug script that has been written quickly and effectively. The problem with using `alert` is that you must ensure all alerts are removed or commented out if being used for tests or debugging. This is due to them being very obvious to users if they are not removed, and some do find them rather irritating to have to keep clicking away.

I tend to like testing in this way for initial development because of how easy it is to use. However, alert does not provide an ongoing testing method, so it can be better to put in a cleaner logging method for maintenance of your code.

Jslog

Another way of testing and debugging client-side scripts is using `jslog`. When using `jslog`, you can write lines in scripts to send logs to the JavaScript log. The JavaScript log can be opened in the developer system settings so that messages can be viewed. This method will only show logs to users who have the JavaScript log open, so it can be a less intrusive method of testing scripts.

The contents of a `jslog` message can be the same as a message using `alert`. Let's have a look at how we write this in script:

```
jslog('Testing Message');
```

In the preceding example, the message `Testing Message` will appear in the JavaScript log. Jslog can contain strings or variables, but it will not display in the ServiceNow logs. It only appears in the JavaScript log, so you must ensure you have it open if using this testing method.

As the JavaScript log will not be open for regular users, it is possible to leave these logs in for future maintenance of scripts. If you choose to do this, make sure that the logs you leave in are well documented and minimal. It is difficult for a new developer to maintain an instance they are new to, where the JavaScript log is constantly being updated.

Browser

The browser method is not a ServiceNow-specific way of debugging client-side scripts, but can be a useful one. Because these scripts are running on the client, web browsers often have ways of displaying running JavaScript code that you can check.

These methods vary based on the browser you use to view ServiceNow, but most modern browsers will have some way of checking what JavaScript is running which can be used to test your client-side scripts.

I personally tend to like using Google Chrome for browser-based testing, but other browsers can be just as good.

Script examples

Having introduced the basic elements of client-side scripting and how and where to use it, we can take a look at some examples of scripts to further our understanding.

We'll start by looking at some client script examples.

In this first example, we'll use an onLoad client script to show and hide form sections based on the logged-in users' roles. We'll only show the related records form section on the incident form if the logged-in user has the itil_admin role:

```
function onLoad() {
    if (g_user.hasRole('itil_admin')) {
        g_form.setSectionDisplay('related_records', false);
    }
}
```

As you can see in the example, we are using g_user's hasRole method to determine whether the logged-in user has the required role. If they don't, then we use the g_form setSectionDisplay method to hide the form section. Putting this client script as an onLoad type allows us to ensure that this form section is immediately hidden from the user.

I have often used this type of script before to hide sensitive data that appears on a form section. This can range from financial details to personal information held by HR.

We can see how this script would look in *Figure 3.6*:

Figure 3.6: OnLoad client script to hide form sections

Now let's have a look at an onChange client script example. Sometimes, we may want to increase the speed at which incidents for certain categories are looked into. Let's suppose that for this example, we want to set the urgency to high for all network incidents, medium for database ones, and low for all other users.

We need to make sure we set the Field name field value to Category for our onChange script. Let's look at the code we need:

```
function onChange(control, oldValue, newValue, isLoading, isTemplate) {
    if (isLoading || newValue === '') {
        return;
    }

    switch(newValue) {
        case 'network':
            g_form.setValue('urgency', 1);
            break;
        case 'database':
            g_form.setValue('urgency', 2);
```

```
        break;
    default:
        g_form.setValue('urgency', 3);
    }

}
```

In this example, we have used a `switch case` statement to perform different actions, based on the new value of the field. This JavaScript technique is more efficient than using multiple `if` statements. We have also used the `newValue` parameter that ServiceNow gives us to quickly decide on which value we should set the urgency to.

When setting the value of the urgency in this example, the user is still able to amend the urgency field if they feel the urgency is not fitting for this particular incident. It is possible to lock down fields though which have been populated by scripts by making them read-only or setting security rules.

Let's take a look at how this client script looks in *Figure 3.7*:

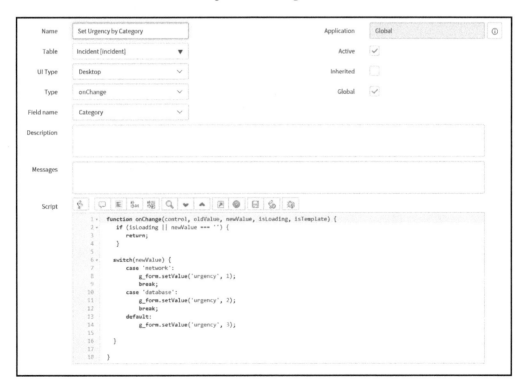

Figure 3.7: OnChange client script setting urgency based on category

Next, we'll have a look at an example using an `onSubmit` type client script. These are less used than some of the other types of client script, but it is good to see how to create one if necessary.

In this example, we'll look at making sure a user has filled in the description if they have the `itil` role. Sometimes you may want to ensure that users with more technical experience fill in further information on a form:

```
function onSubmit() {
    if (g_user.hasRole('itil') && g_form.getValue('description') == '') {
        g_form.addErrorMessage('Enter a description to save.');
        return false;
    }

}
```

In the preceding example, we use the `g_form.addErrorMessage` method to show a message at the top of the form if a user with the `itil` role tries to save the form with no description. This message will let the user know why they are not able to save the form. The code that stops the record from being saved is returning false from the `onSubmit` function. If at any point in the `onSubmit` script the function returns false, then the record will not be saved.

Being able to stop a form from being saved is an important aspect of the `onSubmit` type of client script, and arguably, its main use.

The example we have scripted can be seen in *Figure 3.8*:

Figure 3.8: OnSubmit client script enforcing description update for itil users

Now let's see an example using the `onCellEdit` type of client script. Often, these types of script are used to validate the input that a user enters into a cell on the list view.

For this example, we will ensure that a user does not enter a high impact into a cell to force them to open up the form view to do this:

```
function onCellEdit(sysIDs, table, oldValues, newValue, callback) {
  var saveAndClose = true;
  if (newValue == 1) {
    alert('High Impact cannot be set on a list view.');
    saveAndClose = false;
  }
  callback(saveAndClose);
}
```

This example uses the `newValue` parameter to check the value the impact has been set to. If it has `high` or `1` as the value of the field, which we need to use in scripts rather than labels, then the user is alerted through a message. By setting the `saveAndClose` variable to `false`, we can also stop the field from being updated. This is because the callback is using this variable, and therefore also sets the `callback` to `false`.

Often, business rules can be used to fulfill a similar task to the `onCellEdit` scripts, but it is useful to see how they can be created.

We can also see how this script looks in ServiceNow in *Figure 3.9*:

Figure 3.9: OnCellEdit client script stopping impact being set to high on list views

These examples give us a good understanding of the different types of client script, and some uses for each. Now we'll take a look at UI policies.

As a UI policy is configured, we mainly only need to use script if we want to run scripts for the **Execute if true** and **Execute if false** fields we described earlier in the chapter.

For this example, we will change the short description when the UI policy condition matches and clear the value again if the condition does not match. Firstly, let's see the **Execute if true** script:

```
function onCondition() {
  g_form.setValue('short_description', 'Matched condition');
}
```

As the condition handles when we want the script to run, we simply need to perform the actions we want to take in the **Execute if true** script. This script will change the value in the short description field.

Now let's see the **Execute if false** script:

```
function onCondition() {
  g_form.setValue('short_description', '');
}
```

This second script will clear the **Short description** field if the condition does not match. In this example, the short description field would only ever contain no value or the `Matched condition` text. When writing scripts in UI policies, think carefully about all of the outcomes of your script. Writing scripts in these two separate scripts can be more difficult, which is why scripting is usually done in client scripts rather than UI policies.

We can see the UI policy containing the scripts we created in *Figure 3.10*:

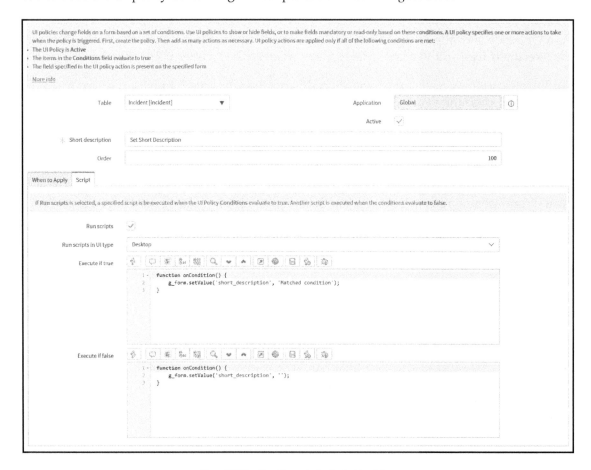

Figure 3.10: UI policy setting or clearing the short description

Summary

During this chapter, we looked at basic uses of client-side scripting in client scripts and UI policies. We explored the four different types of client script and saw how each script type works. We also discovered how and when to write client-side scripts and how to test and debug them. Finally, we looked at some practical examples of client-side scripts and where uses of the different types of client script can be utilized.

In the next chapter, we continue with client-side scripting, looking at the more advanced techniques and areas where client-side scripts can be used. We take a look at script actions, AJAX calls for calling server-side scripts, and using UI actions to run client-side scripts.

4
Advanced Client-Side Scripting

In this chapter, we will explore the advanced side of client-side scripting. Here, we will take a deeper look into scripting on the client and using some of the more advanced techniques that are available.

The topics we will cover in this chapter are:

- UI actions
- AJAX calls
- Advanced client script examples

UI actions

UI actions are generally considered to be a server-side script, but they can also run as client-side script, too. We will cover an introduction to UI actions and their basic usage in the server-side basics in the next chapter. Here, though, we will look at the more advanced techniques of running UI actions on the client side.

Client-side UI actions

To change a UI action to run client-side script, we first need to check the client field tick box. This brings up some additional fields, including the checkboxes to select which list versions the UI actions will be compatible with, but the main new field we are interested in is called `onClick`.

The `onClick` field runs the client code contained inside it when the UI action is selected. Visually, this is only a small field, and not that appropriate for code, so most developers call a function in this field and define the function in the main script field.

Let's look at an example of this usage. For the code in the `onClick` field, we only need to call the following function:

```
onClick();
```

Then, in the script field, we can define the function and contain the code we want to run inside it:

```
function onClick() {
// Write script here to run when an UI Action is selected

}
```

This method of calling a function that resides in the script field is used by ServiceNow UI actions that are provided with the out-of-the-box platform.

We can see what these UI actions would look like in *Figure 4.1*:

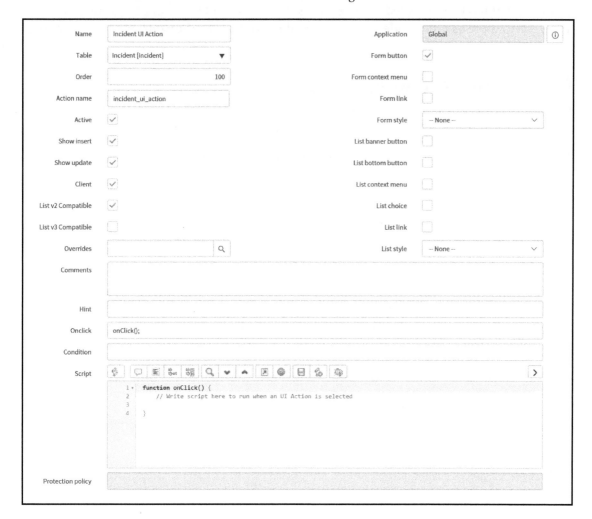

Figure 4.1: Example UI action containing client-side script

In our example in *Figure 4.1*, we can see the UI action as a form button, as that is the checkbox that has been selected. The call in the `Onclick` field to the `onClick` function allows us to write as much code as we need in the script field inside our `onClick` function.

Calling server-side script

Now that we have seen how to use client-side scripts in UI actions, we can look at taking this a step further and using client- and server-side script in the same UI action.

This can be achieved by first calling client-side script in the UI action, which then calls the UI action in the code, and therefore runs the server-side script. This is a slightly strange concept to imagine at first, so let's see how it works.

First, we need to take a look at the line of code that calls the UI action from the client-side code:

```
gsftSubmit(null, g_form.getFormElement(), '<ui_action_name>');
```

The preceding line of code calls the UI action, but this time, it will run it on the server side. When using this technique, you must ensure that the **Action name** field of the UI action is the same as the name referenced in the script. The first argument of `gsftSubmit` is for a control, but seeing as we don't want to use this, we just pass null. This second argument is to get the form; in our case, we just want to get the current HTML form. The third argument is the action name, so this needs to be our UI action action name.

Next, let's look at the server side of the script:

```
if(typeof window == 'undefined')
serverSideCode();

function serverSideCode() {
//Run the server side UI Action code

}
```

The first part of this code is an `if` statement to check that we are running on the server side and not the client side anymore. This little piece of code also ensures that we do not receive browser errors. If the `if` statement evaluates to **true**, we then call a function to run our server-side code.

We can use the preceding example and call the `onClick` function in our script field:

```
function onClick() {
// Write script here to run when an UI Action is selected
gsftSubmit(null, g_form.getFormElement(), 'incident_ui_action');

}

if(typeof window == 'undefined')
serverSideCode();

function serverSideCode() {
//Run the server side code

}
```

This now gives us a UI action that is running client- and server-side code. We will look at some further examples later on in the chapter.

This type of script can be very useful, often being used on the client side to ensure certain fields are filled in or conditions are met before submission and the server-side code is run.

AJAX calls

The AJAX call is a way of calling server-side script from the client side in an efficient way. It is possible to simply use `GlideRecord` on the client side, but this is not considered best practice. It is worth remembering that every time we call the server from the client side, we have to make a round-trip from the client to the server and back again. This takes time and shows as a delay in front of the user. Therefore, we want to reduce the amount of server calls we make, and ensure that any we do are as efficient as possible.

An AJAX call can perform multiple `GlideRecord` queries on the server, which saves us having to perform multiple calls to the server. For the AJAX call to work, we need to have some client-side script and some server-side script. This is most commonly a client script and a script include; we'll look at script includes further in a later chapter.

Client-side AJAX

The client side of the AJAX call needs to set up the AJAX call and pass the relevant parameters to the server side. Once a response is received from the server, we can use the returned value or values to decide what changes to make. Let's have a look at how the client side of the AJAX call works:

```
var ajaxCall = new GlideAjax('serverAjax');
ajaxCall.addParam('sysparm_name','getUserLocation');
ajaxCall.addParam('sysparm_user_id', g_form.getValue('caller_id'));
ajaxCall.getXML(ajaxResponse);

function ajaxResponse(response) {
    var answer =
response.responseXML.documentElement.getAttribute("answer");
    alert(answer);
}
```

The preceding example covers the calling of the AJAX call and the return function, based on the results that are returned. In the first line, we create a new AJAX call and give it the name of our script include. Following on from this, we can add parameters to send to the server. The first one we need to include every time, as the `sysparm_name` parameter is the name of the function we want to call on the server side.

After that, we can send as many parameters as we like to the server side to use in the server-side script. In the example, we are sending the current caller in the `sysparm_user_id` parameter.

Finally, we use a `callback` function, which has the result returned to it using the `getXML` function. This allows the AJAX call to work asynchronously, and the client-side code can continue to run. You can use `getXMLWait` as a synchronous call instead, but this will stop the client from running code until the server-side code has completed, so is not best practice.

In the `callback` function, we make the answer variable the returned value of our server-side code. In this example, we are just showing an alert to the user of the result of our server-side script.

Server-side AJAX

Now that we have seen the client aspect of an AJAX call, let's have a look at the the server-side code that is required to make this work.

As mentioned before, we need to call the script include the same name as our AJAX call and make sure it contains a function with the name in the `sysparm_name` parameter. We also need to ensure we make the script include the client callable for the AJAX call to work, and we can do this by checking the **client callable** tick box on the script include:

```
var serverAjax = Class.create();
serverAjax.prototype = Object.extendsObject(AbstractAjaxProcessor, {
  getUserLocation: function getUserLocation() {
    var userRecord = new GlideRecord('sys_user');
    userRecord.get(this.getParameter('sysparm_user_id'));
    return userRecord.location.getDisplayValue();
  }
});
```

Here, we are using the `getUserLocation` function to return the caller's location back to the client. By using `GlideRecord` and the `get` method to obtain the user record, we can then return the location from that user record back to the client. We are using the display value to display to the user on the client; otherwise, we simply display the location record `sys_id`, which does not mean much to an end user.

By using AJAX calls, we can pass back single values like in our example, or multiple values if needed. An array is a good way to pass multiple values back, but you can use other methods, too, as the response is an XML document.

Script examples

Now that we have seen some more advanced ways of using client-side script, let's look at some examples of how to use these newly learned techniques.

Let's first look at UI actions. We may want to use a UI action to progress states in a change record, but we want to make sure certain fields are filled in before we progress on to other states. We can use client- and server-side code to achieve this. First we use the client-side code to validate the form, and then the server-side code to perform changes to the record.

We can have a look at how this would work:

```
function validateForm() {
  g_form.setMandatory('justification', true);
  //Call the UI Action to run the server side script
  gsftSubmit(null, g_form.getFormElement(), 'authorize');
  g_form.setMandatory('justification', false);
}

if(typeof window == 'undefined')
  setToAuthorize();

function setToAuthorize() {
  current.state = -3;   //Authorize state
  current.update();
}
```

In the example, on the client-side script, we are setting the field we want populated to `Mandatory` in the script to ensure that it is populated before the form is submitted. This is a good way of notifying the user of the additional field to fill in, as it uses the ServiceNow `Mandatory` functionality, rather than popups appearing to the user. You will notice that after the submission, we stop the field being `Mandatory`. This is so that if the user wants to simply save the form or change different field values, they are not stopped by the `justification` field still being `Mandatory`.

For submitting the form, we use `gsftSubmit` and the action name of our UI action, which, in this example, is `authorize`. This allows the server-side script to run our server function, `setToAuthorize`. As the `state` field uses numbers as its values, we set the field to −3, and, as in the example, it is good practice to add comments to let other developers know what the value equates to; and it can be a good reminder for yourself.

We can take a look at what this UI action would look like in *Figure 4.2*:

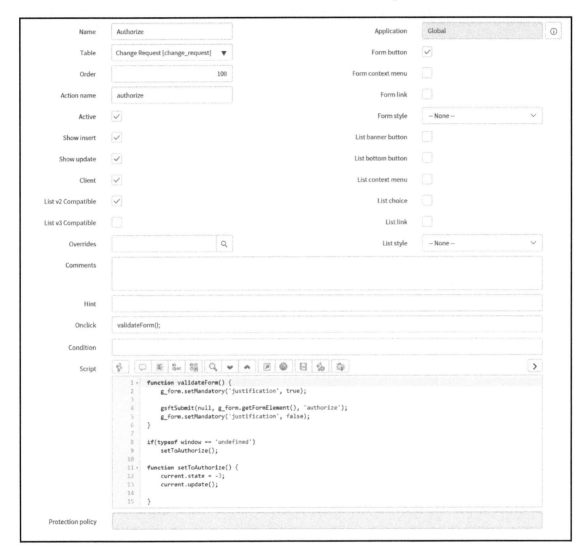

Figure 4.2: Authorizing UI action with client- and server-side script

This method of using client script to validate and server script to perform actions is very useful and works very nicely for UI actions.

Now let's take a look at an AJAX call example. For this example, we are going to look at a catalog item with dependencies on the variables in the catalog item. Sometimes users may have certain access that needs to be revoked, perhaps when they leave the company. When we select the user, we want to ensure that they have some kind of access; otherwise, there will be nothing for them to pick in the remaining fields, resulting in a poor user experience.

Let us take a look at the client-side script we would put into a catalog client script:

```
function onChange(control, oldValue, newValue, isLoading) {
  if (isLoading) {
    return;
  }
  //Clear the Access field when the user changes to ensure a valid
selection is made.
  g_form.setValue('variables.access', '');
  if (newValue == '') {
    return;
  }
  //Ensure a selected user has some active access else clear field
  var ga = new GlideAjax('accessCheck');
  ga.addParam('sysparm_name','userHasAccess');
  ga.addParam('sysparm_user', newValue);
  ga.getXML(AJAXParse);

}
function AJAXParse(response) {
  var answer = response.responseXML.documentElement.getAttribute("answer");
  if (answer == 'false') {
    g_form.addErrorMessage('User has no access to remove.');
    g_form.setValue('variables.user', '');
  }
}
```

This would be put inside a catalog client script as an onChange script, and therefore dictates our function name. When we use catalog items and variables, we have to prefix our variable names with variables and then the variable name to use g_form methods. In the example, we are using a user and access variable, and as you can see, we clear the access variable when the user changes so that we don't end up with a mismatch of data on the screen where a user picks some access and then back fills the user.

Before we initiate the AJAX call, we check that the new value of the user field is not blank. If it is, there is no use making a round-trip to the server, so we use return, essentially exiting the script. If the value is not blank, then we use an AJAX call, calling our script include and sending a user parameter containing the new value in the user field.

When a response comes back from the server, if the result is that the user has no access, then we can assume there will be no access to select and remove for the user. Therefore there would be no selections to pick in the access variable. Rather than give the user nothing to select, we can clear the user field and let the user know the user they selected has no access to remove.

Now that we have taken a look at the client side of this example, let's have a look at the server-side code. Remember that the script include name and function need to match up with the client code making the AJAX call:

```
var accessCheck = Class.create();
accessCheck.prototype = Object.extendsObject(global.AbstractAjaxProcessor,
{
  /**
  * Ajax Call - Returns whether a user has an active access record
  */
  userHasAccess: function userHasAccess() {
    var uAccess = new GlideRecord('u_access');
    uAccess.addQuery('u_user', this.getParameter('sysparm_user'));
    uAccess.query();
    if (uAccess.next()) {
      return true;
    }
    return false;
  }
});
```

In the server script, we are using a GlideRecord to check a custom access table, hence the u_ prefix using the sysparm_user parameter we passed to filter the result down to only records containing that user. If we find a record of access, we return true back to the client and false if no record can be found.

By returning false back to the client-side script, we clear the user variable on the form and show an error message so that the logged-in user knows that the user they selected has no access. If we assume a suitable reference qualifier has been set up, this would stop the logged-in user selecting the access variable after selecting a user and finding no records to select.

Since AJAX calls are so widely used, let's take a look at another example. In this example, we will notify a user on the incident form whether the change they have selected related to the incident that still has open tasks.

This time, we'll use a client script to make the AJAX call. We need it to run when the change request field changes on the incident form, so we'll use an onChange script. Let's have a look at how this client script code will look:

```
function onChange(control, oldValue, newValue, isLoading, isTemplate) {
  if (newValue === '') {
    return;
  }
  //Check whether change request has open tasks
  var ga = new GlideAjax('changeScripts');
  ga.addParam('sysparm_name','changeHasOpenTasks');
  ga.addParam('sysparm_change', newValue);
  ga.getXML(AJAXCall);
}

function AJAXCall(response) {
  var answer = response.responseXML.documentElement.getAttribute("answer");
  if (answer == 'true') {
    g_form.showFieldMsg('rfc', 'Change has open tasks', 'error');
  } else {
    g_form.showFieldMsg('rfc', 'Change has no open tasks', 'info');
  }
}
```

In this example, we see an AJAX call again, this time sending the change request selected as a parameter. We do not need to run the AJAX call when the change field value or newValue is empty, but this time, we do want our script to run on load, so we have removed the isLoading check from the beginning of the script.

When we return from the AJAX call, we are using g_form to show a field message which appears just below the field to show whether the change request selected has open tasks or not.

Now we'll take a look at the server-side script that makes this AJAX call work. A script include will be used to hold the code:

```
var changeScripts = Class.create();
changeScripts.prototype = Object.extendsObject(AbstractAjaxProcessor, {

  /**
   * Ajax Call - Returns whether a change has open tasks
   */
  changeHasOpenTasks: function changeHasOpenTasks() {
    var cTask = new GlideRecord('change_task');
    cTask.addQuery('change_request', this.getParameter('sysparm_change'));
    cTask.addQuery('state', 'NOT IN', '3,4'); //Closed and Cancelled
```

```
      cTask.query();
      if (cTask.next()) {
        return true;
      }
      return false;
    }
  });
```

In the server-side script for this example, we are using a `GlideRecord` to find all the change tasks that are still open for the change request we passed in as a parameter. In the preceding script, we are using an `addQuery` line for the `GlideRecord` where the state is not 3 or 4, which equates to closed and canceled. This allows us to treat any other state as open, even if further active states have been added from the out-of-the-box setup.

This means that if any record is found, we can return `true` immediately, as we only need to know that at least one task is still open. There is no point in running through other change tasks if we find one that is still open, and this keeps the processing time down and the code more efficient.

Once the return value is sent back, the corresponding field message will display to the user using the client-side code. This type of AJAX call can be very useful for giving users extra detail on forms about the data they are entering.

The AJAX call is widely used, and I would certainly recommend becoming acquainted with it as early as possible for scripting in ServiceNow, as many requirements will need an AJAX call so they can be fulfilled.

Summary

In this chapter, we looked at the advanced side of client scripting. We saw how we can use UI actions to run client-side code and run client- and then server-side code. We also took a look at the all-important AJAX call for an efficient way to call server-side code from the client. Lastly, we had a look at some examples of how to use these advanced client-side techniques.

We will move on to the server side in the next chapter and see how to get started writing server-side script. This includes business rules, UI actions, and access controls. We'll also look at when these scripts should be written, how to test them, and some practical examples to help you get started.

5
Introduction to Server-Side Scripting

In this chapter, we will now take a look at the server side of scripting. Here, we look at getting started writing server-side scripts by introducing the basics for producing server-side code. We will also see how to test these scripts and take a look at some examples.

We will be looking at the following topics in this chapter:

- Business rules
- UI actions
- Access controls
- How and when to write server-side scripts
- Testing a server-side script
- Server-side script examples

Business rules

Business rules are usually the most used server-side scripting method. It is possible to use business rules in a basic way that simply requires configuration, rather than customization. I will say that for the majority of requirements that need a business rule, you will most often need to add some sort of customization in the form of scripts.

A particularly helpful aspect of business rules is the different ways they can be triggered. This allows us to run our server-side scripts at different times, based on actions that occur to a record.

When first viewing the business rule form, there are two options for when to run the business rule. These are upon the insert or update of the record. With the business rule in this essentially basic view, we can configure the business rule to run on a filter condition or ownership of a role and change field values. If we want to do more than this, which is often the case, we need to tick the advanced tick box on the form.

Once the advanced tick box has been checked, we then have four options for what action the business rule should run on. Let's look at what these are and when, exactly, they run:

- **Insert**: Runs when a new record is inserted
- **Update**: Runs when a record is updated
- **Delete**: Runs when a record is deleted
- **Query**: Runs when records of this type are searched against

The time that a business rule runs is also dependent on the value of the **When** field. Here, we also have four options to choose from:

- **Before**: Runs before the record is saved
- **After**: Runs straight after the record is saved
- **Async**: Runs when the scheduler runs a scheduled job that gets sent to the scheduled job queue after the record is saved
- **Display**: Runs before the form is loaded, after the data has been fetched from the database

It is best to use before business rules when you are updating the record itself; then the changes are made before the insert or update, and so the record only updates once. After business rules should be used when the script does not affect the current record, so the script can run after a save.

Async will run at some point in the future, so I would only use this if the actions taken in the script do not need to be seen straight away. This can be for queuing up events for notifications or sending jobs out from ServiceNow. Display business rules are best used to hold data in a scratchpad so that a client-side script can utilize it. This is helpful, as it stops client-side script from having to make a round-trip to the server, as the display business rule has already collected the data needed.

Using these checkboxes and the **When** field in combination gives a good selection of triggers for running our server-side script. The most common tends to be a before or after **When** field value with the insert and update checkboxes ticked.

With the advanced box ticked, we can also see the advanced form section. This gives us the condition for running the script and a script field to put our server-side code into.

Now that we've had a look at the form of a business rule, let's have a look at how we add script. All we need to do is set up the form for when we want the script to run, add a condition if appropriate, and add our code in the script field.

As an example, we'll set a network category incident to a high impact when created. For this, we need to add a condition in the **condition** field:

```
current.category == 'network'
```

This **condition** field is helpful to stop running through scripts when it is not necessary. In the preceding code, we will only run our script if the category is network.

Now we'll look at the script we will run:

```
(function executeRule(current, previous /*null when async*/) {

    current.impact = '1'; //High Impact

})(current, previous);
```

First, let's look at the code ServiceNow gives us for a business rule. The executeRule function we are provided with has two parameters: current and previous. current is the object that holds all the current values of the record when the business rule is triggered. previous is the object that holds the value of the record before any updates were made, essentially holding the previous values. Previous can only be used with the update and delete actions.

Our example sets the impact to high for network category incidents. For our example, we would set the **When** field to **before**, which means we do not need to add any script to update the record, as we are changing the current record before it is being saved. We also need to check the insert checkbox on our business rule. We can see the business rule itself in *Figure 5.1*:

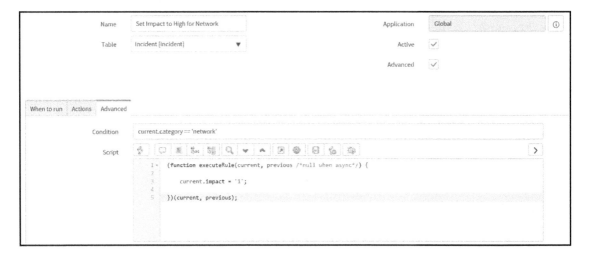

Figure 5.1: Business rule setting a high impact for network category incidents

This gives an overview of how business rules work, and they are very well used across the ServiceNow platform.

UI actions

UI actions are the buttons, context menu selections, links, and list selections that you find throughout ServiceNow. Because you can make UI actions appear in different areas of the platform, they can be incredibly handy to add your script to.

I tend to find that the form buttons are most used for UI actions. These can be added as helpful additional buttons to add functionality or ways to move records through different states of a process.

A UI action normally runs on the server side; however, we can run them on the client side, too, as we explored in the client-side chapters. By using the tick boxes, we can run UI actions on an insert when the record is created or on an update once the record already exists.

First, let's take a look at the different ways you can display a UI action to the user. By ticking the relevant checkboxes, a UI action you create can be displayed in one or multiple ways. Let's have a look at these options:

- **Form button**: This displays the the UI action as a button on the form, similar to the **Update** button
- **Form context menu**: Displays the UI action in the context menu, the menu that appears when you right-click the header bar of the form
- **Form link**: Displays the UI action as a link in the related links section, which appears between the form sections and related lists
- **List banner button**: Displays the UI action as a button at the top of a list view, next to the table label
- **List bottom button**: Shows the UI action at the bottom of a list as a button
- **List context menu**: Displays the UI action in the list context menu, accessed by right-clicking in a list of records
- **List choice**: The UI actions appear in the choices of actions on selected rows at the bottom of the list
- **List link**: Shows the UI action in the related links section at the bottom of a list

In a similar way to business rules, we also get a condition and script field for UI actions. However, the script field starts blank on a UI action, so the developer must provide all of the code.

We'll take a look at scripting a basic UI action. For our example, we'll build a form button to change an incident state to `In progress`. Let's take a look at the code we need:

```
//Moves the incident state to In progress
current.state = 2; //In progress
current.update();

action.setRedirectURL(current);
```

In the preceding code, we set the state to the value of 2, which corresponds to the `In progress` state for incidents. Once this value has been set, all we need to do is update the record using `current.update`.

The `action.setRedirectURL` line is used in UI actions to redirect to the current record once the server-side script has run. If no redirection code is used when a UI action is pressed on a form, it will move back to the previous screen, usually the list view the record was selected from.

In our script, this redirection line is saying that once the code has run, redirect the page to somewhere different; in our example, we use current as the current record. This then redirects back to the record we are on. This is helpful if we want to keep the user on the same record and show them the changes our UI action has made. In this case, the user should be able to see the state change.

We can see the UI action in *Figure 5.2*:

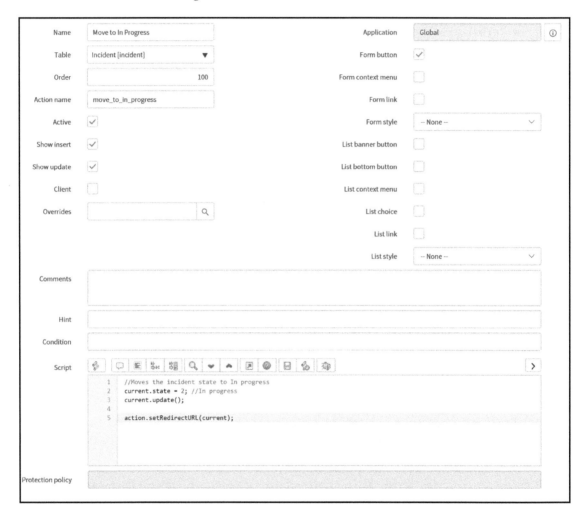

Figure 5.2: UI action that moves the state field to In progress

Here, we are only using our UI action as a form button, but we could also display it in other ways by using the tick boxes on the right. This UI action will appear on new and existing incident forms with the **Show insert** and **Show update** tick boxes checked.

Access controls

Access controls are a security aspect of ServiceNow, and whether access is given is mainly governed by configured roles. However, if a more complex calculation as to whether users are allowed access is required, we need to use script to account for this.

Generally, access controls are defined without the need for scripting, but there are still a fair amount of scenarios that require code to be used. These are often when information about a user is needed further than their roles; for example, their group membership or company.

To amend access controls, you need to have the **security_admin** role and ensure that you elevate privileges and use it before trying to make changes to them. To get to the scripting aspect of an access control, you need to tick the advanced checkbox. Once this is done, the script field will appear at the bottom of the form.

For each access control, a user is only granted access if they match all three aspects of the access control: the role, condition, and script. This is worth remembering when writing your access scripts, as it could be a role or condition stopping access, rather than the code you have written.

Now let's take a look at some access control code. Here, we will allow write access to the task number field if the user is part of the current assignment group:

```
gs.getUser().isMemberOf(current.assignment_group);
```

This example will allow the user access if they are a member of the current assignment group. The script in an access control needs to set an answer variable to true or false, or simply evaluate to true or false. In the example, we are just using the evaluation method.

In *Figure 5.3*, we can see the whole access control, allowing write access to the task number field. This would apply to task tables; for example, incident, change, and problem:

Figure 5.3: Access control for the Number field on the Task table

Access control scripting can be fairly short, and you tend to not get such complicated code here, but getting the right code is very important, as access controls can become a very complicated area of ServiceNow, with many rules applying and not applying to grant or disallow access for users.

How and when to write server-side scripts

Server-side scripting is generally preferred to client-side scripting, so it should be used where possible. As server-side script tends to run away from the user frontend, it is less likely to affect loading times that a user would see as a poor user experience.

That said, it is still advisable to configure before customizing and avoid scripting at all, wherever possible. This is because script is harder to maintain and is more likely to cause issues between releases of ServiceNow.

Let's explore some common uses for server-side scripting and how to best achieve these tasks.

Changing form values

Changing form values is usually best achieved by a business rule or UI action. If you want to change values when a user makes a click, then a UI action is best; however, if you simply want the values to change at all times when certain conditions are met, then a business rule is better. It is best to use a before business rule so that the form is only updated once.

Restricting access to forms and fields

When restricting access to forms and fields, it is best to use an access control. An access control will restrict access no matter how a form is accessed, so it is a powerful tool. If you only need to use roles or conditions to control access to forms and fields, then that is the preferred method, as this is classed as configuration and is easier to maintain.

If your access requirements are more complicated or convoluted than this, though, you will need to add script to the access control. The most common reasons for this are that a user needs to be part of certain groups or the user is referenced in fields on the form.

Passing values to the client side

Sometimes, you may want to pass values to the client side because they will not be visible on the loaded form, and these values may be useful for running client scripts. In this instance, you will want to use a display business rule. This allows scratchpad values to be set in the display business rule, which can then be used in client-side script on the form.

If you are considering calling the server from an `onLoad` client script, then it is usually better to use a display business rule instead, as this eliminates the need for an extra call to the server.

We can see what a display business rule looks like in *Figure 5.4*:

Figure 5.4: Display business rule example

It is worth noting that once we pick the **When to run** field as display, we no longer have the **Insert**, **Update**, **Delete**, or **Query** checkboxes available to select. This is because a display business rule always runs at the same time, just before the form is loaded.

Review

We have looked at a few examples of when to script on the server and the best way to do it in various scenarios. Server-side scripting is usually much more common than client-side scripting and accounts for the majority of code in most ServiceNow instances.

Therefore, we are really just beginning to look at the possibilities of server-side scripting. There is great potential in the code that can be written, and we will explore some more advanced methods in the following chapter.

Testing server-side scripts

As with client-side scripting, there are a few ways to test server-side scripts. These are generally less immediate than the client-side debugging techniques, but essential when working to fix your code.

gs.log

The first logging technique we will look at is `gs.log`. This was a very popular technique, and still is fairly widely used by developers. As we saw in Chapter 2, *Exploring the ServiceNow Glide Class*, `gs.log` lets us send logs to the system log with a script source so we can send messages as a piece of code executes.

We can create a `gs.log` from any server-side script, which makes it very useful; however, we cannot use it in a scoped application. We will have a look at scoped application logging later. As long as you are in the global scope, you can use `gs.log` and send messages to the system logs.

Let's remind ourselves of a simple piece of code using a `gs.log`:

```
gs.log('Server Side Log Message');
```

This log will appear in the **Script Log Statements** module in the application navigator when the script runs. We can also show the values of variables at certain stages in a script using this method. We could use this to display the caller on an incident record:

```
var user = current.caller_id;
gs.log('The current caller is ' + user);
```

This would display the current caller of an incident in the logs if used in a business rule. We can use the plus symbol to add strings and variables to our logging.

This method allows us to add as many logs as we like to our scripts to check that methods were called or the values of variables at certain points in the code.

Remember to remove all of your `gs.log` statements or comment them out before putting your code live. Leaving too many logging lines in code can make the system logs difficult to debug.

Logging in scoped applications

As we discovered when we looked at `gs.log`, it does not work in scoped applications. For logging in scoped applications, we need to use a different method. In fact, there are four methods that can be used.

The four levels of logging in a scoped application are:

- `Error`
- `Warn`
- `Info`
- `Debug`

This type of logging works in a very similar way to `gs.log`, but with the different levels of log replacing the word `log` after `gs`.

Let's have a look at how to write a basic script for each:

```
gs.error('Error log');
gs.warn('Warn log');
gs.info('Info log');
gs.debug('Debug log');
```

These logs are visible in the application logs table, which can be viewed by going to **System Logs** | **System Log** | **Application Logs**.

By default, when you create a new application scope, only error, warn, and info messages are displayed, as set by the system property related to the scope. This property will be named `<scope name>.logging.verbosity` and can be set at any of the four levels. For each level set, it will show messages at that level and any higher-level message types. As the default value for the property is info, we will see all messages, apart from debug.

In general, a lot of developers will simply use info messages as a generic way to debug script on the server side. However, if you are building debugging into the scoped application being created, it is better to use all of the level types for a more complete solution.

Session debug

ServiceNow also provides some server-side debugger assistance in the form of session debugging. These are mainly listed as modules in the **System Diagnostics** application, but there is also security debugging available in the **System Security** application.

By clicking on these modules, you activate the debugging for that particular area; for example, business rules. This lasts for the session, or until you turn the debugging off by using the **Disable All** module.

I have found that these modules can be useful, mainly for the security rule debugging, but are not generally comprehensively used by developers.

Script debugger

The script debugger has been introduced in the Istanbul release for use in server-side scripting. This allows developers to set break points in any server-side script, to then step through in the debugger.

To use the debugger, you must first click the left margin in a script to create a break point. Then, to load the script debugger, navigate to **System Diagnostics** | **Script Debugger**. The script debugger appears in a new window, where you can see the break points created in the script, as in *Figure 5.5*:

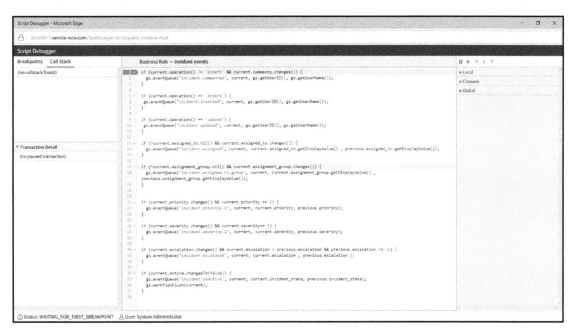

Figure 5.5: Script debugger stepping through the incident events business rule

Once the debugger is opened, trigger the script, and you are given the option to **Start Debugging,** which will allow you to step through the script.

This can be a helpful tool if you need to find out where issues are in a script and are unsure of where in the script the problem lies. This is also a good tool for longer scripts often housed in script includes.

Script examples

Now that we have seen how the basics of server-side scripting work, we can take a look at some scripting examples to further our knowledge of how to use these introductory server-side techniques.

We'll start with a further business rule example.

This time, we will create a before delete business rule to ensure that directors are not deleted. We need to set the business rule to advanced; select the **delete** checkbox and **before** in the **When** field. Let's have a look at the code:

```
(function executeRule(current, previous /*null when async*/) {

    if (current.title == 'Director') {
        gs.addErrorMessage('Cannot delete Director');
        current.setAbortAction(true);
        action.setRedirectURL(current);
    }

}) (current, previous);
```

Here, we are checking whether the user is a director using the **title** field, and if so, using `setAbortAction` to stop the `delete` going ahead. To ensure the user is kept informed, we are also using `addErrorMessage` to display a message to the user and `action.setRedirectURL` to keep the user on the current record, so that they can see that the `delete` did not go ahead.

The rule can be seen in *Figure 5.6*:

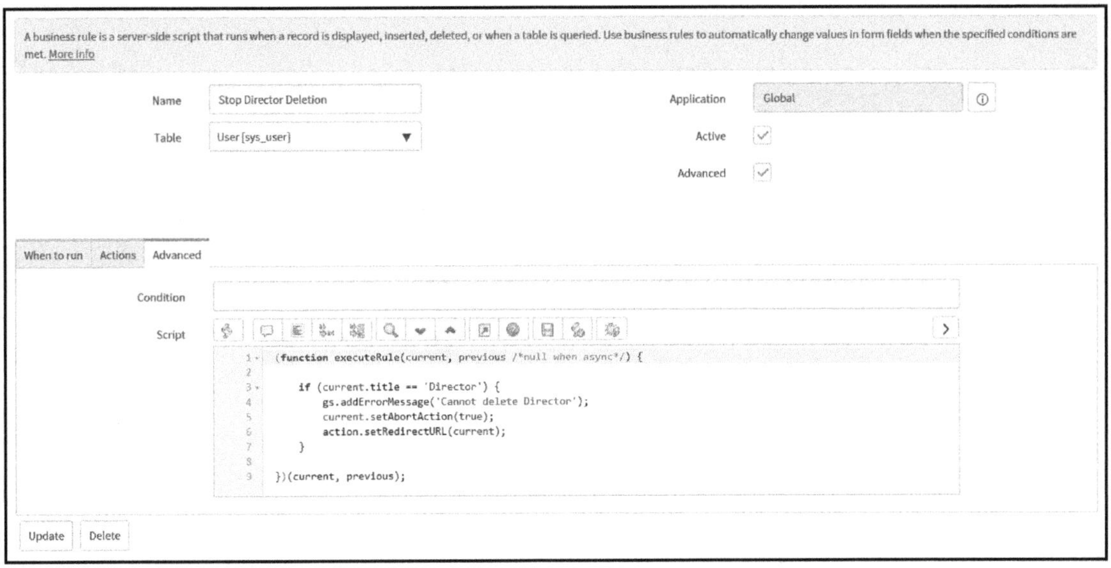

Figure 5.6: Business rule to stop director deletion

Next, we'll take a look at a UI action example. For this UI action, we will make a button to assign an incident to ourselves. Firstly, we will add a condition to only make the button appear on the form if it is a current member of the assignment group:

```
gs.getUser().isMemberOf(current.assignment_group)
```

This line ensures that the logged-in user is a member of the assignment group, so that the incident can be assigned to them. The code we need to assign the incident to the user looks like this:

```
//Assign to the current logged in user
current.assigned_to = gs.getUserID();
current.update();
```

The two lines set the assigned to value of the incident to the current logged-in user and then update the record to save the changes. This is quite a simple UI action, but one that is very helpful.

Here, in *Figure 5.7*, we see the UI action we created:

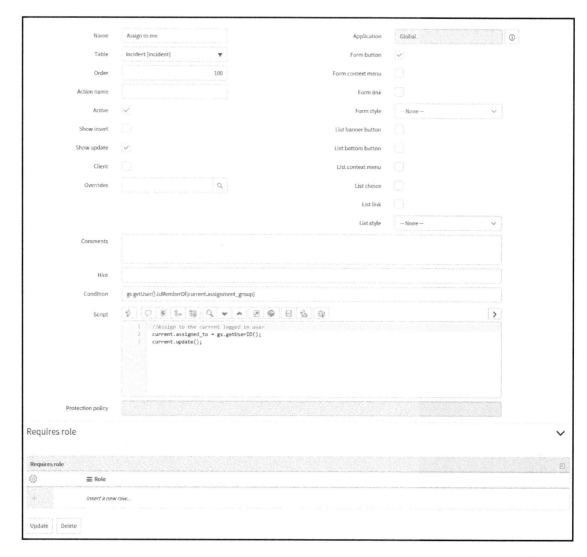

Figure 5.7: UI action to assign an incident to the logged in user

Often with UI actions, the script may not need to be that long to be an effective solution and add value to the user.

Finally, we will take a look at an access control script example. Sometimes it may be necessary to restrict access to a single group and exclude even system admins from seeing records.

We will use the change request table for this example, but obviously, other read access controls exist that would need to be deactivated for our new access control to work. We will only allow the eCAB Approval group access to Software category changes.

Let's take a look at the code:

```
answer = false;
  if (current.category == 'Software') {
   if (gs.getUser().isMemberOf('eCAB Approval')) {
     answer = 'true';
   }
} else {
    answer = 'true';
}
```

Here, we are allowing access if the category is not Software; or, if it is Software, the user must be a member of the eCAB Approval group. We are clearing the **Admin overrides** checkbox, so even an admin will need to adhere to the rule to gain access. We also add the itil role to the rule to ensure that this role is needed for access to be given.

We can see the rule that we have created in *Figure 5.8*:

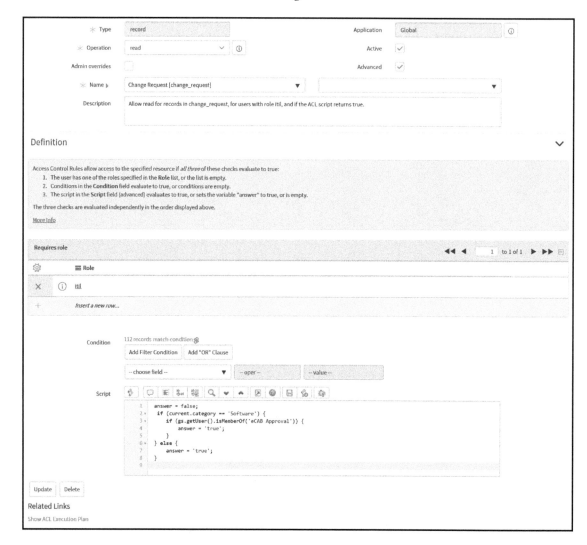

Figure 5.8: Access control to restrict access to the Software category to eCAB Approval group members

This type of access control can be useful for sensitive information that perhaps even a system admin may not be able to view.

Summary

In this chapter, we looked at the basics of server-side scripting through business rules, UI actions, and access controls. We saw the various different runtimes of business rules and the multiple ways a UI action can be displayed to the user. We took a look at when it is appropriate to write server-side script and some examples of common uses, as well as how to test server-side script. We also saw some practical examples of server-side scripting using learned techniques.

In the following chapter, we will be looking at the advanced side of server-side scripting, including script includes, scheduled jobs, and background scripts. We will also look at how to script in workflows and script actions, as well as how to set up events. We will introduce these server-side advanced topics and show you some practical examples.

6
Advanced Server-Side Scripting

In this chapter, we will be taking a look at the advanced side of server-side scripting. We will explore some more advanced methods and techniques that can be used on the server side, building upon what we learned in the previous chapter.

In this chapter, we will take a look at the following topics:

- Script includes
- Scheduled jobs
- Background scripts
- Workflow scripts
- Event management
- Script actions
- Advanced server script examples

Script includes

Script includes are at the heart of scripting in ServiceNow, and are arguably the most commonly used when it comes to writing code. Script includes are used to hold classes of code, and for a lot of the backend script used by the ServiceNow platform.

When creating your script include, you first need to give it a name. This name will be important, as it will be used in other code to call the methods in your script include.

 Ensure that the name you choose for your script include does not contain spaces in it. It is best to use underscores to separate words in the name.

Once you enter a name for your script include, you will notice that the **API Name** and the **script** fields are populated. The API name is read-only, and given based upon the name of the application this script include is being created in, followed by the name of the script include itself.

The script field is populated with some introductory script creating a class for this script include, taking into account the name of the script include. As an example, if we named our script include `script_utils`, we would be given the following script:

```
var script_utils = Class.create();
script_utils.prototype = {
    initialize: function() {
    },

    type: 'script_utils'
};
```

This gives us the basic code to create a script include class that can be called from the server side. One of the first questions to ask when creating a script include is whether the script will be called from the server side only, or from the client side. This is because if we are going to be calling the script include from the client side (for example, for an AJAX call), we need to tick the **Client callable** checkbox, and in doing this, you will also notice that the code changes, too.

For our example, this will change the code to the following:

```
var script_utils = Class.create();
script_utils.prototype = Object.extendsObject(AbstractAjaxProcessor, {

    type: 'script_utils'
});
```

This changed script allows the script include to inherit the `AbstractAjaxProcessor`. Without this, AJAX calls will not work, so it is important to remember this if the script include will be called on the client.

Although this is the starter code that ServiceNow provides for you, it is not necessary to create a class in a script include. You can also simply create a function to call in a script include when calling server-side script.

Let's look at a short example of how that can be done:

```
function script_include_test() {
   return 'Test Complete';
}
```

This is a simple function that will just return the string of text, but can be called simply as a standalone function, rather than creating a whole class.

Let's now have a look at creating a script include with a class and methods. We can add as many methods as we like to our script include:

```
var script_utils = Class.create();
script_utils.prototype = {
   initialize: function() {
   },
   testMethod: function testMethod() {
      return 'Method completed successfully';
   },
   type: 'script_utils'
};
```

Our `testMethod` method will return a string when called on the server side. To call it, we use the line of code as follows:

```
new script_utils().testMethod();
```

We can also assign this line of code to a variable or use it for a condition check if the method returns true or false.

Script includes can also call each other and methods contained within them. When building up the bulk processing of server-side script, it is usually best to consider script includes for the job. Looking at the existing script includes that come with the ServiceNow platform is a good way to enhance your knowledge of writing script includes.

Scheduled jobs

Scheduled jobs are a way of generating a report or record and automatically running a script. Creating a report or record is a configuration and does not require scripting. What we are interested in for scheduled jobs is the ability to automatically run a script.

A scheduled job is a helpful way to run a script at a time of your choosing. This can be an overnight job or a script that can run frequently, say, every hour. In my experience, running script out of hours is one of the main benefits and uses of a scheduled job. Common uses are preparing data for users first thing in the morning, or to remove old data.

When creating a scheduled job, we set the frequency of the scheduled job by using the **run** field. The different time options in this field give the developer different fields to fill in to schedule the script execution appropriately. If the **On Demand** option is picked, the script will only run if the **Execute Now** button is pressed.

In addition to the schedule, we can also add a condition to the scheduled job so that it will only run when the condition evaluates to true. If you check the **Conditional** checkbox, then an additional **Condition** field is displayed. For the script in this **Condition** field, the final expression of the code needs to evaluate to true or false.

Let's have a look at an example of a condition script for a scheduled job:

```
var dateTime = new GlideDateTime();
dateTime.getDayOfWeek() != '7'
```

In the example, we are checking if the current day is Sunday, and if so, we will not run the scheduled job script. The `getDayOfWeek` method gives us the day of the week, with one being Monday and seven being Sunday.

The second line of script above can give a syntax error saying that a semicolon is missing and an expression is seen when a function call or assignment was expected. Normally this would be valid, but for the condition field in a scheduled job we are expecting an expression and adding a semicolon here would cause the script to break.

Now let us look at the **Run this script** field. This is the field where we put the code that we would like to run at the scheduled time we have defined.

For an example, let us log that our code has run and that it is not a Sunday:

```
gs.log('Today is not Sunday');
```

We can write any server-side script we like in this field to run at the specified time. We will look at a more advanced example later in the chapter.

We can see what our scheduled job will look like if we set it to run daily at 1:00 a.m. in *Figure 6.1*:

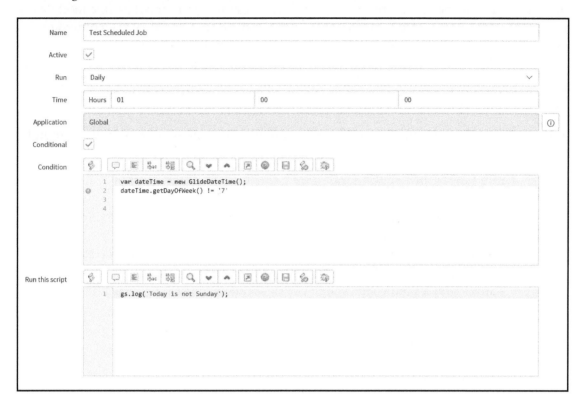

Figure 6.1: Scheduled job to check if the day is Sunday

A scheduled job is a great way to run script-performing server-side tasks out of business hours.

Background scripts

Background scripts are server-side scripts that administrators can immediately run on the ServiceNow platform. A background script cannot be saved and does not exist as a record. However, they can be extremely useful for trialing scripts out and fixing one-off issues with an instance.

To start creating a background script, you simply need to select the **Scripts - Background** module in the **System Definition** application. This brings up a large box for the developer to write their code into. If you have administrator access and you cannot see the module, there is a system property that can be set that means an elevated privilege is required to access background scripts. If this is the case, this usually means you need the **security_admin** role to access background scripts.

Because background scripts grant the ability to run any JavaScript on the platform, this module is often locked down more securely for security purposes.

There are a few choices and buttons that appear under the large script box for background scripts. These are:

- **Run script** (button): Runs the script currently in the **Run script** box on the server side
- **in scope** (drop down): Allows the background script to be run in a different scope outside of global, if required
- **Execute in sandbox?** (checkbox): Executes the script with sandbox restrictions; for example, data cannot be inserted, updated, or deleted
- **Cancel after 4 hours** (checkbox): Check to cancel the script if it is still running after four hours

Let's look at an example of a background script:

```
var inci = new GlideRecord('incident');
inci.addQuery('category', 'software');
inci.query();

while (inci.next()) {
  gs.log('Incident ' + inci.number + ' would be deleted');
  //inci.deleteRecord();
}
```

In the example, we are checking for all of the incidents that have the software category. In the background script, we are logging each incident we find so that we can review the list before we go ahead with the deletion. Once we are happy with the list that will be deleted, we will see in the log that we can remove the log and remove the comment lines, allowing the deletion to take place.

This type of example is useful when performing a large removal of records to gauge the impact before going ahead with the script.

Let's have a look at what the background script will look like:

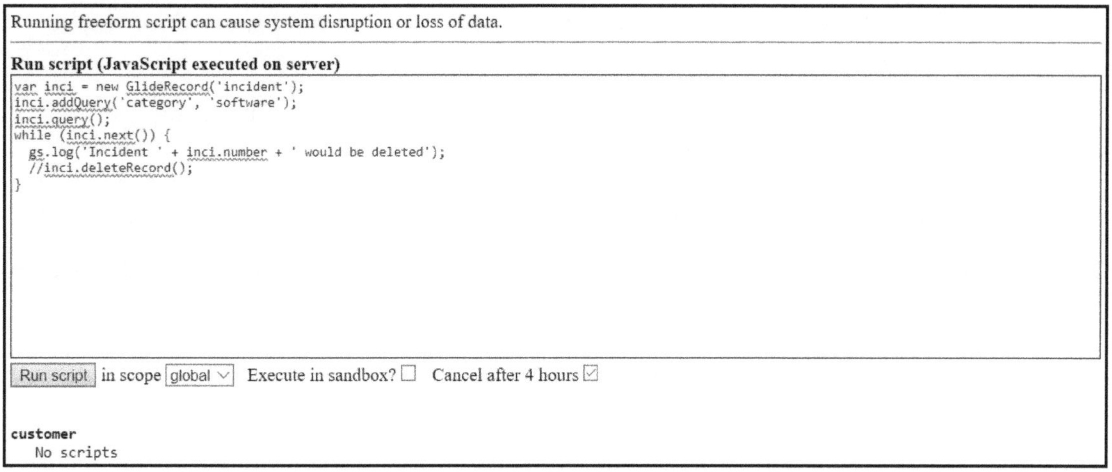

```
Running freeform script can cause system disruption or loss of data.

Run script (JavaScript executed on server)
var inci = new GlideRecord('incident');
inci.addQuery('category', 'software');
inci.query();
while (inci.next()) {
  gs.log('Incident ' + inci.number + ' would be deleted');
  //inci.deleteRecord();
}




 Run script  in scope global    Execute in sandbox?    Cancel after 4 hours

customer
  No scripts
```

Figure 6.2: Background script to log records for deletion

Background scripts are very helpful for running script to check results before performing actions, and also to test parts of a script involved in a long process so the process does not need to be walked through each time to test the code.

Workflow scripts

Workflows use a number of activities to build up a process in ServiceNow. These activities can often be used on a basic level, without the need for scripting. However, to build a more advanced workflow, we can use code to enhance the workflows we build.

Scripts can appear in a number of workflow activities, including approvals and task creation. For approvals, it is possible to add users and groups to approval activities using script. In task creation, we can use script to set values on our task before it is created.

The main area for scripting in a workflow, though, is in the **Run Script Workflow Activity**. This activity allows the developer to run any server-side script they like at a point in the workflow. This can be used to manipulate records, kick off integrations, or perform other outcomes using scripts.

The other area of workflows in which you often come across scripts is in setting up approvals. A simple approval workflow activity will simply pick a user or group to approve, or perhaps the value of a particular field. However, if you require the selection of relevant approvals to be more complicated than this, then you may need to use some code.

With scripts, you can add extra elements to who will be selected to approve, for example, by checking attributes about the users approving, or the record being approved. It may be that if a record has a particular category, it is sent to a certain approval group, or that the approver of the record must have a certain role. This type of functionality is achievable with script and can cater for many other scenarios too.

The potential for building a complex approval system is huge, but be careful to make sure that what you create provides value and can be maintained.

Let us have a look at an example of a workflow script in a **Run Script Workflow Activity**:

```
//Adds urgent to the short description if the priority is critical
if (current.priority < 2) {
  current.short_description = current.short_description + ' URGENT';
  current.update();
}
```

In the example, we are adding URGENT to the short description of the record if the priority is critical. We also have access to the current record in the workflow script, with the current record being the one from which the workflow launched.

Let us have a look at what this activity will look like, in *Figure 6.3*:

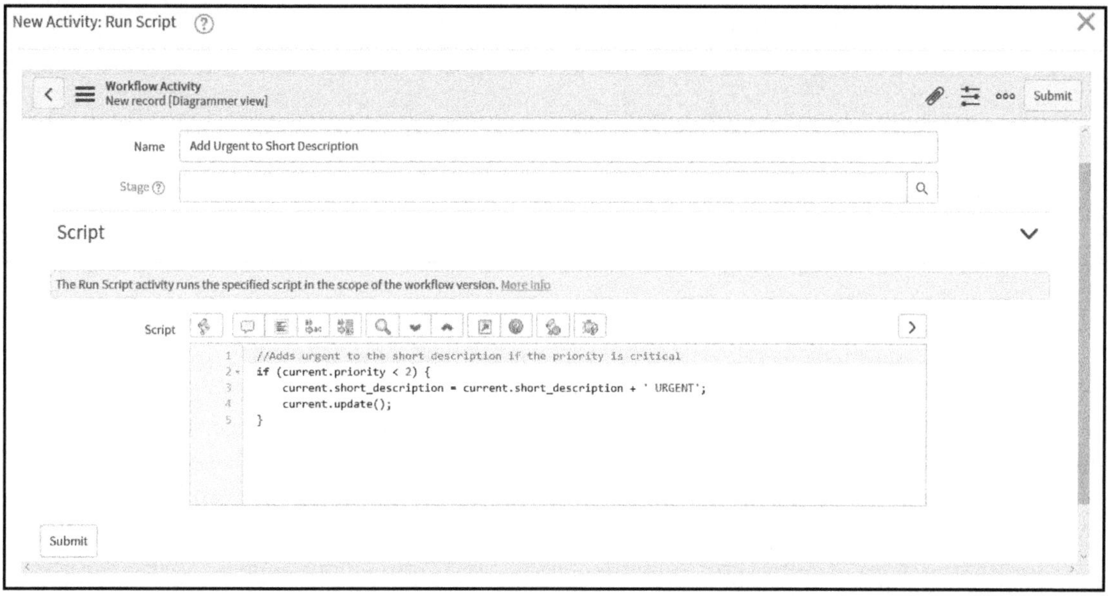

Figure 6.3: Workflow activity to update the short description based on priority

Workflow script can be particularly handy for adding an extra layer of functionality to your workflows. Sometimes, when you look at the activities available, you cannot find one that will meet your requirements, and in this instance, scripting can be the solution.

Event management

Events that trigger different outcomes in an instance run in ServiceNow. An event can be invoked from any script on the server side. The main outcome from an event being triggered is either a notification or a script action. Notifications are usually emails, and we will take a look at script actions later on in this chapter.

First of all, to trigger an event, the event will need to be defined. To define an event, we can navigate to **System Policy** | **Events** | **Registry** and click on the **New** button. Upon doing this, we are given the form shown in *Figure 6.4*:

Figure 6.4: New event form

In the form, we need to give the event a name. Event names are usually words split by full stops and underscores, and if you look at the list of events, you will see the general format used for events. It is also good practice to fill in the table field for reference. The **Fired by** and **Description** fields are simple text fields, but it is a good idea to fill these in with details of when the event should be fired and how the event is fired. Then, the event can be used by others or its trigger point easily found by another administrator.

Once we have defined an event, we then need to be able to call the event to add it to the event queue. We can use the `GlideSystem` method `eventQueue`, as shown in the following code:

```
gs.eventQueue("custom.event", current, gs.getUserID(), gs.getUserName());
```

In the preceding code, we would be calling the event `custom.event`, and this would need replacing with the name of the event you have created. The second, third, and fourth parameters are an object and two strings, respectively. The second parameter is almost always the current record, so that the current record data can be used once the event is processed. The third and fourth parameter are more commonly known as **Parm1** and **Parm2**. These can be used in scripts or in notifications; for example, you are able to send an email to the value held in **Parm1**.

In the example, we are sending the current logged-in user's ID and name. The information sent in these parameters often changes, and is often about the current user or a value that is useful once the event has been processed.

We can also use the `GlideSystem` method `eventQueueScheduled`, which is very similar, except the fifth parameter is the time at which the event should run. This can be set as the value of a field that is of `glide_date_time` type.

We can see an example of this in the following code, using the same event from before:

```
gs.eventQueueScheduled("custom.event", current, gs.getUserID(),
gs.getUserName(), current.dateTimeField);
```

Once an event has been triggered, it will be processed fairly quickly, unless it has been scheduled for a certain time, and the events that have been processed can be seen in the event logs. To see the event logs, navigate to **System Logs** | **Events**. From here we can see the events processed, the processing time, and events still to be processed.

Events provide a great way to process multiple scripts or send notifications based on a single event, and because an event can be triggered in any server-side script, the ways in which an event can be triggered are almost limitless.

Script actions

Script actions tend to be some of the lesser-used methods of server-side scripting. They are run after an event has run in the system scheduler. This can be helpful as a way to run some script at a set point in the future.

There are some system events that will already exist in ServiceNow that you can use to run your script actions from, or you can create your own events and execute them from any server-side script.

When creating a script action, you need to pick the event to run the script action against. This is picked from a list, so make sure the event exists before you create the script action. There is also the option to add a condition script, which is written in the same style as a business rule. You can also perform condition checks in the main script, but if you can use the condition script, it is considered better.

Let's have a look at a script action in use. The main script field can run any server-side script. Here, we will add a simple log:

```
gs.log('Approval Inserted');
```

This example will send a log to the system logs to say that an approval has been inserted. This is fine as an example or for debugging, but would not be recommended as a script for a production instance, as many approvals are created, and this would swamp the logs with this message.

Let's have a look at the script action itself, shown in *Figure 6.5*:

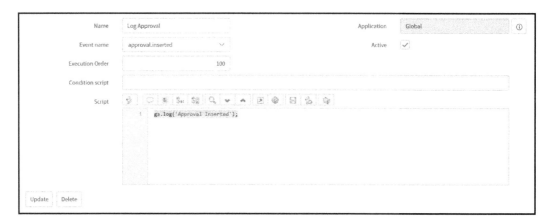

Figure 6.5: Approval-logging script action

Script actions can also be used to set an action to be performed in the future; for example, keeping a record on hold until a certain time in the future.

Script examples

The advanced server-side techniques we have seen can be used in a number of ways, and you will find advanced server-side scripting to be some of the most common in the ServiceNow platform.

Now that we have seen where to write our advanced server-side code, we can have a look at some further examples to solidify our understanding.

Let's have a look at a script include example first. We will write a script to return the active tasks of a requested item. This can be helpful for letting users know which tasks need to be completed for an item to be fulfilled.

First we will take a look at the script include code:

```
var item_utils = Class.create();
item_utils.prototype = {
    initialize: function() {
    },
  getActiveTasks: function getActiveTasks(item) {
    var tasks = [];
    var task = new GlideRecord('sc_task');
```

```
        task.addQuery('request_item', item.sys_id);
        task.addActiveQuery();
        task.query();
        while (task.next()) {
          tasks.push(task.number.toString());
        }
        return tasks;
      },

        type: 'item_utils'
    };
```

We are using the getActiveTasks method to get all of the active tasks returned to us, passing in the item parameter as the requested item record to get the tasks for. Using a gliderecord query, we can find all of the tasks, and are returning them as an array.

In the example, we have started the creation of an item utilities script include. You will often find these in ServiceNow instances having been developed by other developers. We have created the first method here, but you would usually build up more methods for requested items as part of this class to keep the code organized.

We can see what the script include will look like in *Figure 6.6*:

Figure 6.6: Item utilities script include

Now that we have the script include, we need to call it from another location. Here, we will do this from a business rule, and simply log the result. You can use this type of script include to assist in whether to close out requested items, too.

Here is the code for the business rule to call the script include:

```
(function executeRule(current, previous /*null when async*/) {

    var tasks = new item_utils().getActiveTasks(current);
    gs.log('Active tasks for ' + current.number + ' are ' +
tasks.toString());

}) (current, previous);
```

We would run this business rule on the requested item table. In the code block, we put the value of the script include into the tasks variable. We also pass the current requested item record using `current`. We are just logging the output here, but this data could be used for other uses.

Let us also see what the business rule would look like, in *Figure 6.7*:

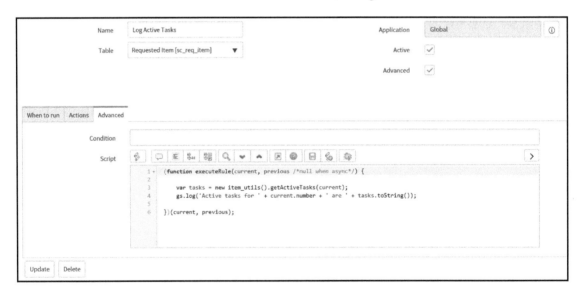

Figure 6.7: Business rule to log active requested item tasks

Now, let us have a look at a further example of a scheduled job.

For this example, we will look at deleting all incidents that are over a year old. This kind of example shows how we can remove old records overnight for different tables.

Let us have a look at what the code would look like:

```
//Delete incidents that have not been updated in the last year.
var date = new GlideDateTime();
date.addYearsLocalTime(-1);

var delIncident = new GlideRecord('incident');
delIncident.addQuery('sys_updated_on', '<', date);
delIncident.deleteMultiple();
```

In this code, we get the current date and time by initiating a new `GlideDateTime` class, and then removing a year from this time. By using a negative number, in this case `-1`, we subtract a year from the current date and time. Using a `GlideRecord` query, we are finding all of the incidents updated over a year ago, and deleting them using `deleteMultiple`. This deletes all of the records without the need to query the `Gliderecord`.

This type of overnight job can be great for clearing out old records or performing updates, ready for the day ahead.

Figure 6.8 shows what the scheduled job itself looks like:

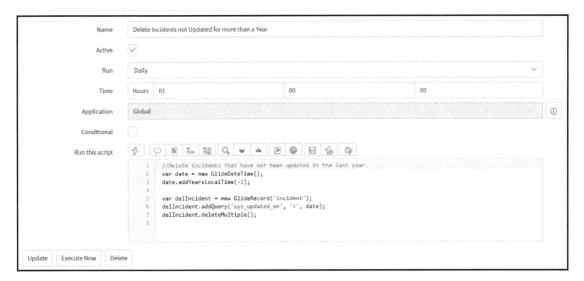

Figure 6.8: Scheduled job to delete old incidents

As you can see in the preceding figure, this scheduled job would run at 1:00 a.m. and delete the incidents overnight. This is common practice so that system resources are not being used during the working day.

It is also best practice to run long-running scripts overnight so that they do not impact the instance resources during business hours. There are also jobs that run overnight written by ServiceNow included in a brand new instance; for example, the `import set deleter`, which cleans up import sets after seven days.

Running overnight scripts is a great way to use scheduled jobs. This can be useful for cleaning up old data or setting up reports so that they are available to users first thing in the morning.

Now, let us have a look at a workflow script example.

Here, we will use an approval activity to add an approval that is the director in charge of the current caller. This involves iterating through managers of users in the database until we find one that is a director.

Let us take a look at the code:

```
var manager = 'current.caller_id.manager';
var title;
while (eval(manager) != '') {
  title = manager + '.title';
  if (eval(title) == 'Director') {
    ans = manager + '.sys_id';
    answer = eval(ans);
    break;
  }
  manager = manager + '.manager';
}
```

In the example, we use the `manager` string to keep adding `.manager` to until we find a user that is a director. This means saying the manager of the manager of the manager, and so on, until a director is found. We can execute this in a loop to save time and resources by using `eval`.

`eval` evaluates the contents of the brackets, rather than treating it as its current type: in this case, a string. This allows us to dot walk to find the title of the user and get the `sys_id` if we find a director. It is also how we can use a loop here, adding `.manager` to the string each time we run through the loop. `eval` can be very helpful when using script to find the field you require, and then to evaluate it once it is found.

If no director is found, then no approval will be added at this stage in the workflow, as when we get to the top of the organisational tree we would meet a user with no manager and exit the loop.

We can see the approval activity from the workflow in *Figure 6.9*:

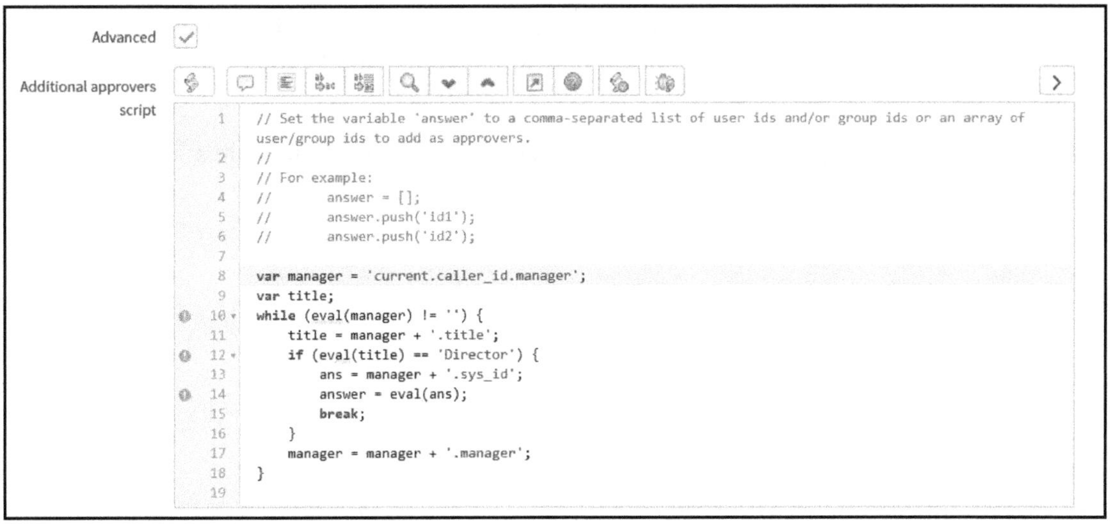

Figure 6.9: Approval activity to find and add the user's director as an approver

For our final example, we will take a look at a script action.

Sometimes we want to put an incident on hold, but incidents can get left on hold for extended periods of time. In this example, we will create a new field to hold a date and time for the incident to stay on hold until. Once the date and time are reached, an event fires which will run our script action and take the incident off hold and move the state to in progress.

To achieve this goal, we also need to set the event to be scheduled in the future. Here, we will use a business rule to do this. The code we will need looks as follows:

```
(function executeRule(current, previous /*null when async*/) {

    gs.eventQueueScheduled("incident.off.hold", current, current.sys_id,
gs.getUserName(), current.u_on_hold_until);

})(current, previous);
```

In the business rule, we are using the `GlideSystem` method `eventQueueScheduled` to put an event into the system scheduler. We have set the third parameter, or what can be referenced as `event.parm1`, in later scripts to be the `sys_id` of the current incident. You will also notice that the final fifth parameter is the value of our custom field to hold the date and time we want the incident to stay on hold until.

This method sets an event into the system scheduler which will run the event at the time we have set in the custom **on hold until** field. The event we are firing (`incident.off.hold`) is a custom one we have created for this particular functionality.

Once the event fires, we need to move the incident out of the **on hold** state and into in progress. For this, we are going to use our script action.

The code in our script action is as follows:

```
var incident = new GlideRecord('incident');
incident.get(event.parm1);
incident.state = '2';
incident.u_on_hold_until = '';
incident.update();
```

We are using the `event` parameter we set in the business rule to use `gliderecord` to get the incident record we want to update. Once we have the record, we can change the state to in progress, with a value of two, and reset the **on hold until** field before updating the incident record.

We can also see the full script action in *Figure 6.10*:

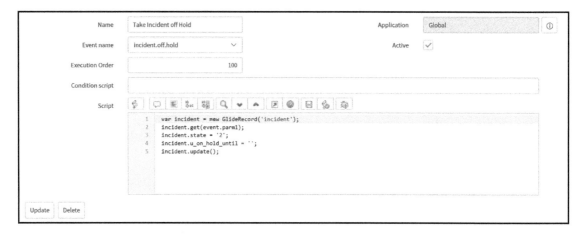

Figure 6.10: Script action to take an incident off hold

This combination of business rule and script action is a very useful technique to know for having the ability to run scripts at a specified time in the future.

These practical examples are great for reinforcing the understanding of these more advanced server-side script techniques.

Summary

Advanced server-side scripting was the theme for this chapter. We looked at the greatly used script includes and scheduling scripts using scheduled jobs, events, and script actions. We also saw how to write script as part of ServiceNow workflows and how to test aspects of our code using background scripts. We finished off with some great examples of how to use these advanced server-side techniques.

In the next chapter, we look at building your own custom pages by utilizing UI pages. We introduce Jelly script and where it appears in ServiceNow, as well as show some examples of creating simple custom pages.

7
Introduction to Custom Pages

For this chapter, we are going to take a look at building custom pages. This will also introduce scripting in Jelly code, and where and when to use it. We will also take a look at how to build a custom UI page.

We will look at the following topics while introducing custom pages:

- Introduction to Jelly
- UI pages
- Custom page examples

Introduction to Jelly

Jelly is certainly a lesser known language to script in. It does not appear in the majority of ServiceNow, only on the outskirts of the platform. However, if you want to create custom pages in ServiceNow, it is a must to learn.

It is unfortunate that Jelly is a lesser known language, as documentation on how to use it is therefore also in short supply. Using pages already created in Jelly or the ServiceNow community can be very useful when getting started due to this general lack of information in the developer space.

One of the main areas you will find Jelly script is in UI pages, which we'll take a look at later in the chapter. Jelly code is found in XML field types, as it is a Java and XML scripting engine that allows XML to be turned into executable code.

When looking at Jelly script, you will see that it is almost always started and finished with the same tags. Let's have a look at this code:

```
<?xml version="1.0" encoding="utf-8" ?>
<j:jelly trim="false" xmlns:j="jelly:core" xmlns:g="glide" xmlns:j2="null"
xmlns:g2="null">

</j:jelly>
```

This code sets up the XML version and encoding, and then the Jelly tags are written. Trim sets whether the whitespace inside this tag should be trimmed, and we set this to false. The other four attributes set up the tags and phases for the Jelly script.

Jelly is split into two phases of processing. The first phase tags are j and g, with the second phase being j2 and g2. In the first phase, the j and g tags are parsed, with the result being cached, followed by the second phase of the j2 and g2 tags. When the script is run subsequently, only the second phase will be parsed again, using the cached data for phase one.

This means that it is a good practice to set data that is unlikely to change in the first phase with constantly changing data in the second phase. The j tags are native to Jelly and the g tags have been created especially for ServiceNow.

Jelly is a necessary skill to learn for creating UI pages and we will look further at how to script in Jelly in the next chapter.

UI pages

UI pages are pages of script and XML that exist all across the ServiceNow platform. There are many UI pages that you will see as you navigate through ServiceNow, including the home pages for the service catalog and knowledge. UI pages are also a way to make custom pages where you can define everything that appears on the page.

Let's look at creating a new UI page. We start by giving our UI page a name; make sure you make a note of the name, as it will be needed to reference the page later on. The category field is mainly for reference and does not provide any additional functionality. It can be helpful for grouping your UI pages.

There are three fields that can contain code in a UI page; they are:

- **HTML**
- **Client script**
- **Processing script**

The **HTML** field is where the Jelly script is held, and ServiceNow provides the tags for you to start your Jelly coding:

```
<?xml version="1.0" encoding="utf-8" ?>
<j:jelly trim="false" xmlns:j="jelly:core" xmlns:g="glide" xmlns:j2="null"
xmlns:g2="null">

</j:jelly>
```

These are the standard tags we saw when introducing Jelly scripting, so we can start to add our Jelly script inside the Jelly tags.

The **Client script field** is a script field that client-side code can be written inside of. This client-side code runs when the UI page is loaded. This script could be put into the **HTML** field, but it is easier to read if separated out into the two fields.

The **Processing script** field is a script field as well, but this field runs server-side script. The script runs when the page is submitted, so is helpful when creating forms on a custom page.

UI pages can be accessed from anywhere in ServiceNow by adding the name of the UI page and .do onto the end of the instance URL. This means that you can navigate to a UI page you create very easily.

Let's have a look at a simple UI page to show how written code appears in the UI page. Here is the code in the **HTML** field:

```
<?xml version="1.0" encoding="utf-8" ?>
<j:jelly trim="false" xmlns:j="jelly:core" xmlns:g="glide" xmlns:j2="null"
xmlns:g2="null">
Sample UI Page Text
</j:jelly>
```

With this code, we will simply see the text **Sample UI Page Text** on the screen of our UI page. We can also add some code to the client script field to see when this is run:

```
alert('Page loaded');
```

We will just use an `alert` here, as we are scripting on the client side to show when the code runs.

Our whole UI page definition can be seen in *Figure 7.1*:

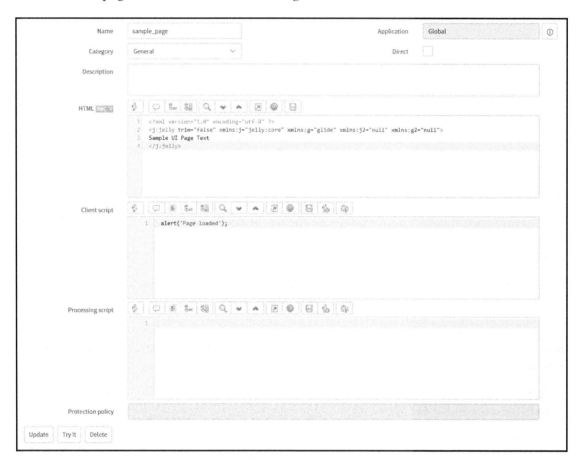

Figure 7.1: Sample UI page definition

We can also take a look at how this page would look by navigating to `sample_page.do`, as shown in *Figure 7.2*:

Figure 7.2: Sample UI page example

UI pages are a great way to create custom pages and move away from the standard ServiceNow form and list layouts seen across the platform. They also give you the opportunity to create a page truly from scratch, containing whatever information and data you like.

Script examples

Now that we have seen how to create a custom page, let's have a look at an example of how to make a working UI page.

For our example, we will create our own change interceptor. This is usually seen when creating a new change, but for the example, we will create a UI page to be the page navigated to.

Here is the code we will use in the **HTML** field:

```
<?xml version="1.0" encoding="utf-8" ?>
<j:jelly trim="false" xmlns:j="jelly:core" xmlns:g="glide" xmlns:j2="null"
xmlns:g2="null">
<nav class="navbar navbar-default" role="navigation">
<div class="container-fluid">
  <div class="navbar-header">
    <input type="HIDDEN" id="sysverb_back"></input>
    <h1 style="display:inline-block;" class="navbar-title">Change Request
</h1>
  </div>
  <div class="nav navbar-right">
  </div>
</div>
</nav>
<div class="container-fluid" style="border-bottom: 1px solid #ddd; margin-
bottom: 5px;">
  <h4 class="wizard-row-indent">What type of change is required?</h4>
</div>
<div class="container-fluid wizard-container">
  <a href="change_request.do?sysparm_query=type=standard">
  Standard Change - A predefined change. </a><br/>

  <a href="change_request.do?sysparm_query=type=normal">
  Normal Change - A regular change with over two weeks until start.
</a><br/>

  <a href="change_request.do?sysparm_query=type=emergency">
  Emergency Change - A change occuring within two weeks. </a>
</div>
</j:jelly>
```

Here, we have used HTML tags to create our own interceptor in the style of the change interceptor. This makes it easy to change aspects of the page in any way we want to, rather than having to use the ServiceNow interceptors module.

By looking at the source code of the change interceptor, here we have used code from the actual interceptor to keep the look and feel of the page in line with ServiceNow. It is often good to make your custom pages look like they fit into the ServiceNow platform to give a good user experience.

In our example, we are allowing the user to pick one of three change choices, and then redirecting them to a new change of that type. In the tag creating the link, we can see how the URL changes for each choice. We use `sysparm_query` in the URL to set values on a new form. For our example, we are using this to set the change type.

Let's have a look at the UI page itself in *Figure 7.3*:

Figure 7.3: Intercepter UI page definition

If we wanted to use this page when a change was created, we could amend **Create New module** in the change application to navigate to the UI page by making the module navigate to the URL `change_interceptor.do`.

Let's see what the UI page will look like in *Figure 7.4*:

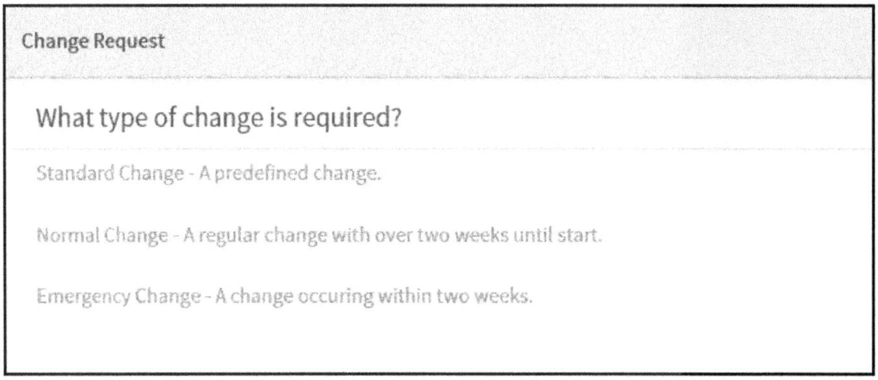

Change Request

What type of change is required?

Standard Change - A predefined change.

Normal Change - A regular change with over two weeks until start.

Emergency Change - A change occuring within two weeks.

Figure 7.4: Intercepter UI page example

We can see the three options we defined on the page with the ServiceNow style navigation header.

Summary

In this chapter, we looked at starting to build a custom page. We introduced Jelly scripting, UI pages, and where Jelly is used inside a UI page definition. We also had a look at a UI page example to see how one is written and how it looks to the user once completed.

In the following chapter, we will explore Jelly scripting more, looking further than the basics. We also introduce UI macros, a way to add reusable components and scripts to UI pages and other areas of ServiceNow. We will also take a look at how we can use UI pages and UI macros together in a practical example.

8
Scripting with Jelly

In this chapter, we are going to look at scripting with Jelly. We will look at how to write Jelly code to create custom pages and scripts to meet your needs. We will also take a look at UI macros and how these are created in ServiceNow, as well as look at an example to further our knowledge in this area.

The following topics will be covered in this chapter:

- Jelly scripting
- UI macros
- Jelly scripting examples

Jelly scripting

Jelly scripting knowledge is important to build custom pages and scripts, and also to amend Jelly code that exists in ServiceNow as part of the platform to work in a different way for your own purposes. We introduced Jelly scripting and how it can be used in a UI page in the last chapter. Let's remind ourselves what the Jelly tags ServiceNow gives us look like:

```
<?xml version="1.0" encoding="utf-8" ?>
<j:jelly trim="false" xmlns:j="jelly:core" xmlns:g="glide" xmlns:j2="null"
xmlns:g2="null">

</j:jelly>
```

Once these tags are in place, we can start to include our Jelly code inside. This can be added to a UI page or UI macro. We will take a look at UI macros later in the chapter.

Evaluate

First, let's have a look at the `<g:evaluate>` tag. This tag allows us to write JavaScript inside the tag and set a variable value at the end, if required.

The `<g:evaluate>` tag is arguably the most used tag in Jelly, and is certainly one to get to grips with. Remember that we can use `g` or `g2` for our tag, depending on which phase we want this script to run in.

Let's have a look at an example of the `<g:evaluate>` tag in action:

```
<g2:evaluate var="jvar_variable">
    var setVariable = 'Set variable to string';
    setVariable;
</g2:evaluate>
```

In the preceding example, we are going to run the code in the second phase, so we are using `g2` in the tag we define. In the tag definition, we are also defining a variable name to use with `var="jvar_variable"`. We can name the variable different names, but we must always prefix the variable with `jvar` for it to work.

Here, we are setting `jvar_variable` to the string value in the script. In an `evaluate` tag, we just need to make the last line of our expression the variable we want to set the evaluate variable to. In our example, we have used `setVariable`, so `jvar_variable` becomes the value of `setVariable`, which is our string.

There are some parameters we can use in a `<g:evaluate>` tag; let's see these used in another example:

```
<g2:evaluate var="jvar_onHoldIncidents" object="true" jelly="true">
    var holdIncident = new GlideRecord('incident');
    holdIncident.addQuery('state', jelly.jvar_onHoldState);
    holdIncident.query();
    holdIncident;
</g2:evaluate>
```

In this example, we can see two new parameters for the `<g:evaluate>` tag: `object` and `jelly`. The `object` tag dictates whether the `jvar` variable should be treated as an `object`. For our example, it would be the `GlideRecord` query, and so we would want this held as an object for later scripting.

The other new parameter is `jelly`. This parameter, if set to `true`, allows us to use `jelly` variables in our script. For our example, we are using the `jvar_onHoldState` variable, which we are assuming has been set to 3 in a previous `<g:evaluate>` tag. We need the `jelly` parameter set to `true` so we can use this variable in our example script.

If

The `if` tag in Jelly script works in a similar way to a JavaScript `if` statement. It is used to run code if a set condition is met. As we can set `if` statements in JavaScript, whether you want to use the Jelly `if` rather than the JavaScript `if` is up to you.

We can use the `if` tag to check whether a `GlideRecord` object has any records inside it. Let's have a look at how this is done using our example from the `evaluate` tag:

```
<g2:evaluate var="jvar_onHoldIncidents" object="true" jelly="true">
    var holdIncident = new GlideRecord('incident');
    holdIncident.addQuery('state', jelly.jvar_onHoldState);
    holdIncident.query();
    holdIncident;
</g2:evaluate>

<j:if test="${!jvar_onHoldIncidents.hasNext()}">
    No on hold incidents.
</j:if>
<j:if test="${jvar_onHoldIncidents.next()}">
    There are ${jvar_onHoldIncidents.getRowCount()} incidents on hold
currently.
</j:if>
```

In our example, we are showing a message depending on whether there are currently on-hold incidents in the instance. The `if` statement has one parameter, which is `test`, which is the expression we need to evaluate to `true` to run the code inside the script in the tag.

This type of `if` statement is helpful to run conditions against `GlideRecord` objects.

UI macros

UI macros are scripts that can be included in UI pages and in other areas throughout the ServiceNow platform. By separating them out from individual UI pages, it makes them easy to reuse across the platform, too.

UI macros are seen throughout the ServiceNow platform, running the service catalog cart and approval summarizers. Let's have a look at how they are created.

A UI macro is quite a simple form, with only a few fields. First, we need to give our UI macro a name. After that, we can add a description, and then complete the XML field. The XML field is an XML type field and works in a very similar way to the HTML field on a UI page. We fill in the XML field with the Jelly script we want to run when this UI macro is run.

We are also given the same Jelly code that we are given when creating a new UI page in the XML field:

```
<?xml version="1.0" encoding="utf-8" ?>
<j:jelly trim="false" xmlns:j="jelly:core" xmlns:g="glide" xmlns:j2="null"
xmlns:g2="null">

</j:jelly>
```

To recap, these tags introduce Jelly scripting, and we can start writing our Jelly script inside the Jelly tags.

We can also invoke a macro from a UI page by using a `macro_invoke` tag. Let's see how this works:

```
<g:macro_invoke macro="kb_article_footer" />
```

We use the `macro_invoke` tag and the macro parameter to invoke our UI macro. We just need to give the name of the UI macro in the macro parameter, as in the preceding example. This example will invoke the `kb_article_footer` UI macro.

It is possible to invoke a UI macro inside a UI macro, too. To do this, we use a `g` tag with the name of the macro inside the tag. We can see how this works in the script:

```
<g:ui_button />
```

This will invoke the `ui_button` inside this UI macro.

UI macros are a great way of writing chunks of Jelly code that can easily be reused throughout the ServiceNow platform. They are especially useful to add to your UI pages.

Script examples

In this chapter, we have seen how to script in Jelly and how to create a UI page ourselves. Let's bring these two abilities together to make a working UI macro.

This is an example of a request I have been asked for before – an approval summary on the group approval record. Here, we need to create a UI macro and a formatter to add to the group approval form.

Let's start with our group approval summarizer code, creating a brief summary of the task record we will be approving with our group approval:

```
<?xml version="1.0" encoding="utf-8" ?>
<j:jelly trim="false" xmlns:j="jelly:core" xmlns:g="glide" xmlns:j2="null"
xmlns:g2="null">
  <tr>
    <td class="label_left" width="100%">
      <label style="margin-left: 12px"> Summary of Record being requested
for approval:
        <g:label_spacing/>
      </label>
    </td>
  </tr>
  <tr>
    <td>
      <table width="100%">
        <tr>
          <td class="label_left" width="150px">
            <label style="margin-left: 10px">Short Description:
            </label>
          </td>
          <td> $[current.parent.short_description]
            <g:label_spacing/>
          </td>
        </tr>
        <tr>
          <td class="label_left" width="150px">
            <label style="margin-left: 10px">Priority:
            </label>
          </td>
          <td> $[current.parent.priority]
            <g:label_spacing/>
          </td>
        </tr>
        <tr>
          <td class="label_left" width="150px">
```

```
          <label style="margin-left: 10px">Opened by:
          </label>
        </td>
        <td> $[current.parent.opened_by.getDisplayValue()]
          <g:label_spacing/>
        </td>
      </tr>
      <tr>
        <td class="label_left" width="150px">
          <label style="margin-left: 10px">Description:
          </label>
        </td>
        <td> $[current.parent.description]
          <g:label_spacing/>
        </td>
      </tr>
    </table>
  </td>
  </tr>
</j:jelly>
```

As you can see, in this example, there is a fair amount of code, but a lot of this is HTML tags, so there is not much real content. In the example, we are creating a table containing some of the details of the record being approved so that the current group approver can see what they are approving.

The labels and spacing are HTML, and you can find this type of script in the UI macros ServiceNow provides for you. The interesting aspect of the code is in setting the task values. We use the dollar sign to declare the start of the variable, then curly or square brackets for phase one or phase two variables, respectively. Here, we are using square brackets to use the second phase, as our data will change and we do not want it to be cached.

We have named this UI macro `group_approval_summarizer`; let's take a look at what it looks like in ServiceNow in *Figure 8.1*:

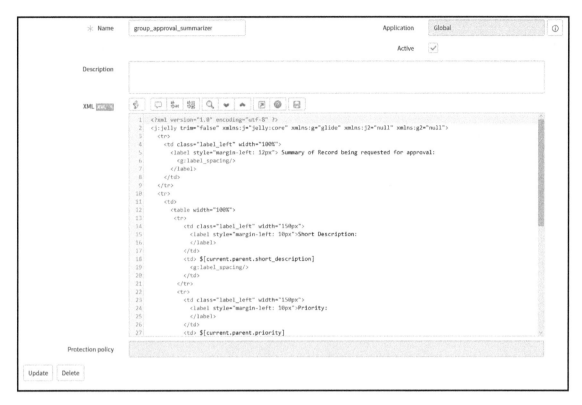

Figure 8.1: UI macro to show a summary of a record being approved

Now that we have our UI macro, we need to build a formatter to link to the UI macro that we can place on the group approval form. The **Formatter** needs a **Name**, a link to the UI macro, and to be on the group approval table. We can see an example of the formatter in *Figure 8.2*:

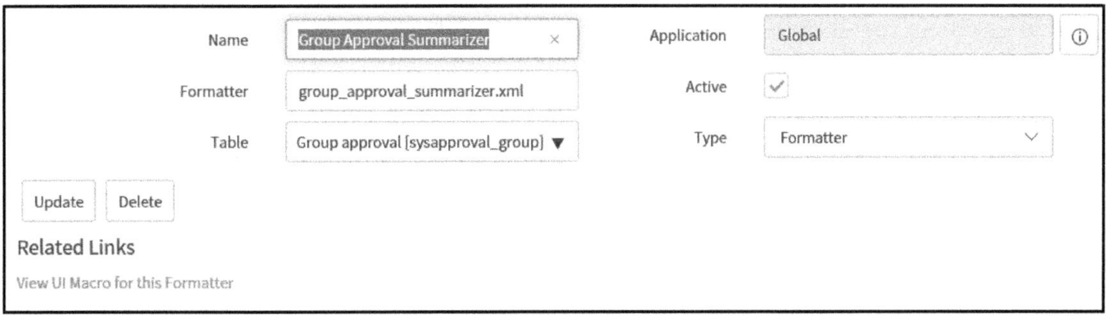

Figure 8.2: Formatter to display a UI macro

Now that we have the formatter, we can add the formatter to the group approval form layout to see our UI macro appear. The results of our UI macro on a group approval form can be seen in *Figure 8.3*:

Figure 8.3: Group approval form with added approval summary

In the preceding figure, we can see the output from our UI macro. This example shows how you can make a UI macro add value to forms in ServiceNow, adding extra data you cannot add with the form layout or designer.

Summary

In this chapter, we looked at scripting in Jelly. We explored the various tags of Jelly and how to use them together to create Jelly scripts. Using these Jelly techniques, we looked at how to create a UI macro containing Jelly script and saw a practical example of creating a UI macro to use in the ServiceNow platform.

In the next chapter, we will look at debugging in ServiceNow. We will look at the debugging tools ServiceNow provides for you in debugging scripts, fields, and the logs you have access to, to help fix errors.

9
Debugging the Script

In this chapter, we will be taking a look at debugging. Debugging is a very important aspect of creating working ServiceNow scripts. We will be taking a look at the script and session debugger, and how these are both used. We will then look at field watchers, debugging applications, the JavaScript log, and debug window. Finally, we will see how to debug REST and SOAP messages in a ServiceNow instance.

In this chapter, we will look at the following topics:

- The script debugger
- The session debugger
- The Field Watcher
- Debugging applications
- The JavaScript Log and Debug window
- Debugging REST
- SOAP debugging

The script debugger

The script debugger allows developers to debug server-side script to discover errors or issues with their code. We had a brief look at the script debugger in `Chapter 5`, *Introduction to Server-Side Scripting*.

To recap, we can set breakpoints in the server-side script we have written to debug the script when it is run by using the script debugger. This is the only way we can use breakpoints in ServiceNow to step through and into our script.

To use the script debugger, we first need to set a breakpoint in one of our server-side scripts. This can be any script you want to step through, either a system script or one you have built yourself. A good example is the `incident_events` business rule, as we can also see how different events are triggered from the incident form, too.

To start, we add a breakpoint in the `incident_events` business rule, as seen in *Figure 9.1*:

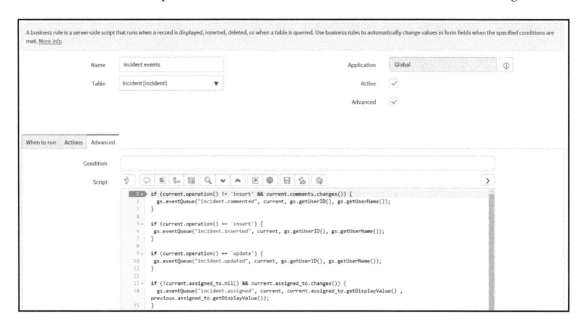

Figure 9.1: Business rule incident_events with break point added

To set this breakpoint, we simply click in the margin of the code to make the breakpoint appear, as shown by the arrow. To remove it, we simply click on the blue arrow, and the breakpoint is removed. Once the breakpoint is set, we can open the script debugger.

To open the script debugger, we can navigate to **System Diagnostics | Script Debugger**. This opens the script debugger in a separate window. We can also open the script debugger from any script type field. We need to click on the script debugger icon that looks like a small insect with a scroll to open the script debugger from this type of field.

We can see this icon highlighted in *Figure 9.2*:

Figure 9.2: Script type field showing the script debugger

We can now run the incident_events script by updating any existing incident, and when we see the window shown in *Figure 9.3*, we click **Start Debugging** to look at the script stopped at our breakpoint:

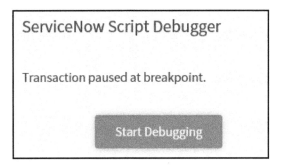

Figure 9.3: Script debugger popup window

Now that we are into the process of debugging, we can switch to the debugging window. From here, we have some fairly standard debugging options that can be seen in the upper right-hand corner of the screen.

We can see these in *Figure 9.4*:

Figure 9.4: Script debugging options

The options we have for debugging are, from left to right:

- **Pause debugging**: The pausing debugger turns the debugger off. This changes the icon to a power icon, but by clicking this changed icon, we can turn the debugger back on again.
- **Resume script execution**: This will resume the script from after the current breakpoint until the next breakpoint, or until the script is complete.
- **Step over next function call**: This button allows you to step through the code and over any function calls, which means skipping over them.
- **Step into next function call**: Clicking this icon steps through the script and into any function called in the code.
- **Step out of current function**: This will step through the current script, but out of any function that the code is currently in.

These buttons allow you to move through the code you have written from the start point of a breakpoint and find where any issues may lie.

This type of debugging is quite typical in a lot of software debugging, with options to pause, resume, and step in, out, and over functions. If this is new to you, however, spend some time familiarizing yourself with these buttons, as it can save you time when debugging longer scripts.

Let's have a look at what the full window looks like in *Figure 9.5*:

Figure 9.5: Script debugging window

This debugging method is very helpful and something that was missing from earlier versions of ServiceNow. With the script debugger, we have a much more rounded debugging experience.

Adding breakpoints in scripts and being able to step through them adds an extra level of debugging, beyond just logging outputs.

The session debugger

The session debugger allows you to debug certain aspects of the ServiceNow platform during the ServiceNow session. You are also able to turn on or off all session debugging. Session debugging will give you a lot of information, but it can sometimes be information overload, so it can be worth picking individual aspects you want to specifically debug. I often find the security debug to be the most useful.

Session debugging is found in system diagnostics and contains a number of modules. You can enable any of the session debugging areas by clicking the module you would like session debugging turned on for. You can also turn on all debugging by selecting **Enable All**. You cannot turn off individual debugging areas, though, except for UI policies, and debugging is disabled by clicking **Disable All** or when the session ends, as well.

We can see the session debug modules in *Figure 9.6*:

Figure 9.6: Session debugging modules

The session debug information appears on each page that you load when information on debugging has been requested, normally at the bottom of the loaded page.

It is also worth noting that it may be that you have to scroll quite far down to see the information provided to you, especially on bigger forms or lists.

A lot of information can be displayed, which can make this method of debugging a little generic, and weaker than a more targeted debugging approach. However, this method of debugging can give information to you that is difficult to find elsewhere in the platform.

Let's have a look at some example session debug output.

First, we will take a look at security. Security in ServiceNow can be a tricky issue to solve if the relevant access is not appearing for the users you are logging in as.

Because is it possible to have multiple access controls for each type of access in ServiceNow, it can be difficult to find the exact rule that is causing issues.

Using session debug, we can see which access controls allowed access and which ones denied it. This can be very helpful in working out whether the access control we are looking at is incorrect and needs to be altered, or if there is an access control we were not aware of that is causing access issues for us.

In *Figure 9.7*, we can see some session debug output for security on the incident form:

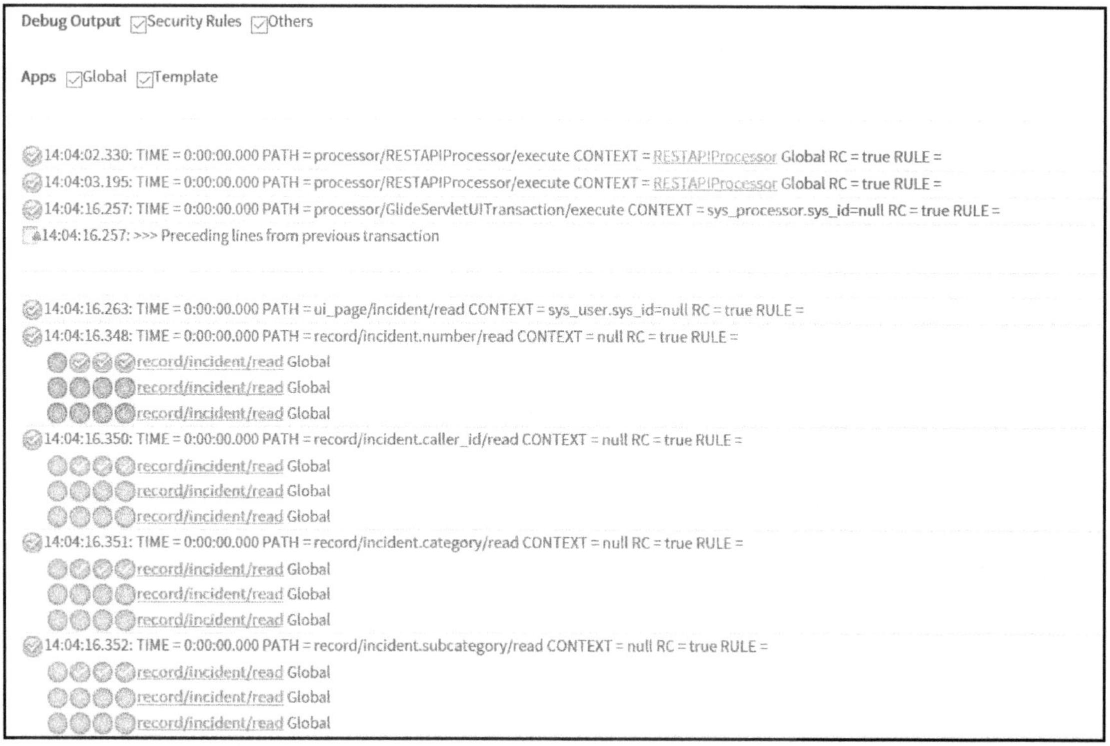

Figure 9.7: Security session debug output

Here, we can see where security rules for the incident form were checked when the incident form was loaded. As you can see, there is a lot of information provided, and this example is only a small section of the session debug information provided for loading an incident form.

The green ticks indicate that the checks against security rules were successful. At the bottom of the example, there are some larger blocks of checks which relate to a specific security check taking place. We can see after **PATH =** the check that is being performed, so, for the bottom check we are looking at **record/incident.subcategory/read**, which means we are seeing whether the logged-in user can read the subcategory field on the incident record. In this case, it is successful, so the field is displayed to the user.

Now, let's see some business rule session debugging.

In *Figure 9.8*, we can see an example of business rule debugging on the incident form:

Debug Output ☑Business Rules ☑Others

14:46:44.665: Execute before query business rules on live_group_member:Created
14:46:44.666: Global ==> 'LiveFeed Group Member Visibility' on live_group_member:Created
14:46:44.667: Global <== 'LiveFeed Group Member Visibility' on live_group_member:Created
14:46:44.667: Global ==> 'LiveFeed Group Member Visibility 2.0' on live_group_member:Created
14:46:44.669: Global <== 'LiveFeed Group Member Visibility 2.0' on live_group_member:Created
14:46:44.669: Finished executing before query business rules on live_group_member:Created
14:46:44.671: Execute before query business rules on live_group_member:Created
14:46:44.671: Global ==> 'LiveFeed Group Member Visibility' on live_group_member:Created
14:46:44.671: Global <== 'LiveFeed Group Member Visibility' on live_group_member:Created
14:46:44.671: Global ==> 'LiveFeed Group Member Visibility 2.0' on live_group_member:Created
14:46:44.671: Global <== 'LiveFeed Group Member Visibility 2.0' on live_group_member:Created
14:46:44.671: Finished executing before query business rules on live_group_member:Created
14:46:44.672: Execute before query business rules on live_group_member:Created
14:46:44.672: Global ==> 'LiveFeed Group Member Visibility' on live_group_member:Created
14:46:44.672: Global <== 'LiveFeed Group Member Visibility' on live_group_member:Created
14:46:44.673: Global ==> 'LiveFeed Group Member Visibility 2.0' on live_group_member:Created
14:46:44.673: Global <== 'LiveFeed Group Member Visibility 2.0' on live_group_member:Created
14:46:44.673: Finished executing before query business rules on live_group_member:Created
14:46:44.674: Execute before query business rules on live_group_member:Created
14:46:44.674: Global ==> 'LiveFeed Group Member Visibility' on live_group_member:Created
14:46:44.674: Global <== 'LiveFeed Group Member Visibility' on live_group_member:Created
14:46:44.675: Global ==> 'LiveFeed Group Member Visibility 2.0' on live_group_member:Created
14:46:44.675: Global <== 'LiveFeed Group Member Visibility 2.0' on live_group_member:Created
14:46:44.675: Finished executing before query business rules on live_group_member:Created
14:46:44.678: Execute before query business rules on sys_user:
14:46:44.679: Global === Skipping 'user query' on sys_user:; condition not satisfied: Condition: gs.getSession().isInteractive() && !gs.hasRole("admin")
14:46:44.679: Finished executing before query business rules on sys_user:

Figure 9.8: Business rule session debugging

In this example section of the business rule session debug script, we can see timestamps for business rule execution and where business rules start and end. The timestamps are to a one thousandth of a second so that the execution order is easier to determine.

Where you can see a ==>, a business rule execution is starting, and a <== indicates the business rule completing. We can also see, in this example, where business rules are skipped due to the business rule condition not being matched, which can be helpful.

Again, the preceding is just a sample of the information given during a load of the incident form with business rule session debugging switched on, so there is quite a lot of data to search through to find what you might be looking for.

Finally, we will take a look at a log session debug.

We can see an example of a log session debug in *Figure 9.9*:

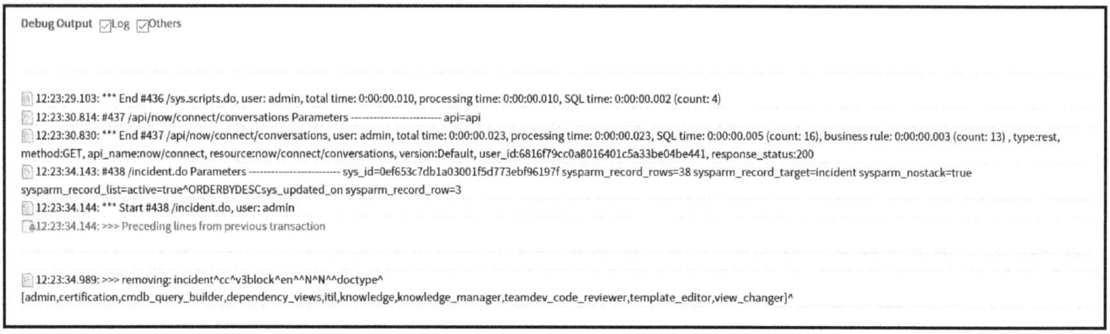

Figure 9.9: Log session debugging sample

The logs will give you logs relating to the opening of the record; in our example, opening the incident form. I do not tend to use this session debugs as much as others, but it can help to track whether any important logs that can lead to information on potential issues occur when records are opened.

The Field Watcher

The **Field Watcher** debugging functionality allows you to watch an individual field and monitor any changes that occur to that field. You can only watch one field at a time using the Field Watcher. If there is a particular field you can see changing, but are not sure what is modifying the value, this can be a helpful tool to use.

To watch a field, right-click on the field in the form view, and at the bottom of the context menu, you should see an option to watch the field. Once this has been selected, a small bug icon appears to show that the field is being watched, and a Field Watcher window appears from the bottom of the frame.

The **Field Watcher** frame shows any changes to the field, and using tick boxes in the **Field Watcher** window, you can switch which type of changes the Field Watcher will check for, for example, business rule, client script, and so on.

A good example to show the Field Watcher in action is to watch the priority field on an incident. If you then change the impact or urgency on the form, you will see the Field Watcher catching the change in the value of the priority field. We can see this in *Figure 9.10*:

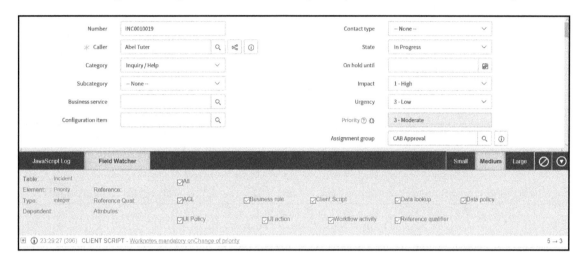

Figure 9.10: Field watcher showing change to priority field

In the preceding figure, we can see that because the **Impact** field was changed to **1 - High**, the **Priority** changed from **5 - Planning** to **3 - Moderate**. This was captured in the Field Watcher and the client script that ran as a result of this change to the field.

The Field Watcher can be a useful tool if you know exactly which field you are interested in and want to know why the value is changing.

Debugging applications

When debugging applications, we are often interested in the scope at given times while our code is running. Some of the tools given to debug applications are actually session debugging modules. We saw the modules, ServiceNow classes as application debugging, along with others, in the session debugging section. These are:

- Debug business rules
- Debug business rules (details)
- Debug security
- Debug scopes

Business rules and security can be useful whether we are in an application or not, but the scope is very important for application coding. To show how debugging the scope works, we can create a test application, and a business rule for that application, in the application scope.

Once the application and the business rule have been created, we need to click the debug scopes and debug business rules modules in the session debugging. As an example, we can see this when updating an incident in the session debug logging.

We can see this in *Figure 9.11*:

```
13:40:46.786: App:Test Application ==> 'Test Application Business Rule' on incident:INC0010019
13:40:46.788: >>>> Entering scope [x_152110_test_appl]
13:40:46.791: <<<< Exited scope [x_152110_test_appl], popped back into [rhino.global]
13:40:46.791: App:Test Application <== 'Test Application Business Rule' on incident:INC0010019
```

Figure 9.11: Session debugging for scopes and business rules

We can see in the logging that, as we enter the business rule from our test application, we also enter the scope of our test application. Once the business rule has completed executing, we revert back to the global scope.

As we saw in `Chapter 5`, *Introduction to Server-Side Scripting*, when we debug using GlideSystem in an application, we need to remember that `gs.log` will not work. For debugging in an application, we need to use four scoped application logging levels.

To recap, these scoped application logging levels are:

- Error
- Warn
- Info
- Debug

These logging levels and their levels of verbosity are helpful to log messages to the system logs when checking values during a script.

We can also enable session debugging for a particular application. This can be enabled from the application page for the related links. Scripts from the application will generate logs to the system log if they use the GlideSystem logging method.

We can see this in *Figure 9.12*:

Related Links

Manage Developers
Publish to Update Set...
Grant app administration to all admins
Enable Session Debug

Figure 9.12: Application related links

To enable session debugging, the **Related Links** needs to be clicked. The related link will change and show as **disable session debug** while the debugging is active. It can be selected again to disable session debugging.

The JavaScript Log and Debug window

The JavaScript Log window is a further way that logs can be viewed in the ServiceNow platform. Rather than using the GlideSystem logging methods, this method allows you to define a different type of log to send to a window that appears at the bottom of the screen.

To see the JavaScript Log window, you can go to the system settings of the instance you are working on. Once displayed, select the **Developer** option. From here, set the **JavaScript Log and Field Watcher** attribute to show the JavaScript Log window.

We can see the attribute set in *Figure 9.13*:

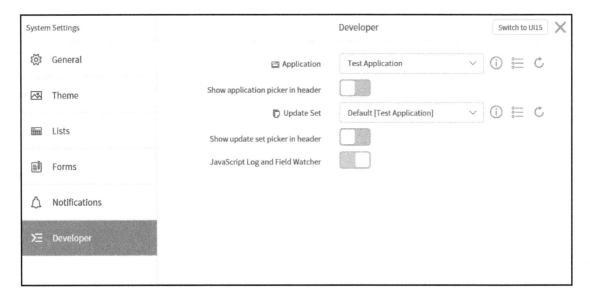

Figure 9.13: Developer system settings showing the JavaScript log and Field Watcher option

Once the **JavaScript Log and Field Watcher** attribute has been set, you will see a window appear at the bottom of the screen. This is the same window that appears to show a watched field, but this time, the tab set will be JavaScript Log.

We can see the window that appears in *Figure 9.14*:

Figure 9.14: JavaScript Log window

This example of the JavaScript window shows no logs, and the window can be cleared from all logging by clicking the circle with a line through it, towards the right-hand side of the header bar.

We can also change the size of the window by clicking on the **Small**, **Medium**, and **Large** buttons in the header bar. The down arrow button in the far-right corner closes the window down.

Logs in the JavaScript Log window are added to the bottom of the list of current logs while the window is open. Logs are timestamped so that you can see which order the logs were added in. This can be especially helpful when looking to see what order client scripts ran in when opening a form in the platform.

To log to the JavaScript Log window, we use `jslog()`, which is a global function. This works in a very similar way to `gs.log`. We can see an example of how to use `jslog` in the following code:

```
jslog('Testing writing to the JavaScript log');
```

If we add the preceding code to an incident `onLoad` client script, we can see the log in the JavaScript Log window.

We can see this in *Figure 9.15*:

Figure 9.15: JavaScript Log with sample log

This method of debugging can be helpful as an alternative to using GlideSystem logs. Some mature instances will sometimes have so many system logs per second, it can be difficult to debug, so this JavaScript Log window can be helpful in this case.

Debugging REST

REST messages are very helpful for integrating between ServiceNow instances and with third-party software. When debugging your ServiceNow instance, you may also need to see logging for REST messages.

To debug REST messages, we need to set the system property `glide.rest.debug` found in the system properties table (**sys_properties**) to `true`. This property may well need to be created, as it is not included in the baseline system.

Let's have a look at an example of this system property:

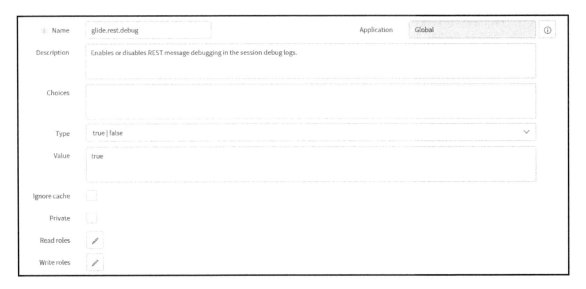

Name	glide.rest.debug		Application	Global	ⓘ
Description	Enables or disables REST message debugging in the session debug logs.				
Choices					
Type	true	false				⌄
Value	true				
Ignore cache	☐				
Private	☐				
Read roles	✎				
Write roles	✎				

Figure 9.16: System property glide.rest.debug

In the example, we can see our created system property. The **Name** needs to be glide.rest.debug and the **Value** set to true. It is also good practice to write a good description with any system property you create, to assist other administrators.

Once this property is set to true, when activating the session debugging debug log we saw earlier on in the chapter, REST message logs will also be added to the log that is output. Once this type of debugging has been completed, this property should be set to false to avoid using up system resources.

SOAP debugging

In a way similar to REST messages, SOAP messages are very important when integrating with other systems. It can be necessary to find out when messages have been received and what exact message came into the instance.

To debug SOAP messages, we need to add a system property, or amend it if it was previously added. The system property that needs to be added is `glide.processor.debug.SOAPProcessor` and the **Value** needs to be set to `true`.

Let's see a completed example of this system property:

Figure 9.17: System property glide.processor.debug.SOAPProcessor

The example shows the system property that needs to be created for debugging SOAP envelopes. The name must be exact, and the value set to `true`. A good description will also help others looking through the system properties to explain its function.

Once this property is set, we will start to see an incoming SOAP envelope XML in the system logs. This is very helpful to see what was received by the instance when messages are received.

Once debugging has been completed, this system property should be set to `false` to stop excessive logging in the instance. This also stops resources from being used to provide these logs when they are no longer being monitored.

Summary

The focus of this chapter was debugging. We looked at the various tools ServiceNow gives us to debug our code and the methods we can use to make the most of them. We looked at the script debugger and making breakpoints, the session debugging modules, and debugging applications. We also took a look at the JavaScript Log and Field Watcher window, and how this can aid us in our debugging.

In the next chapter, we will explore ServiceNow best practices. This includes best practices when writing and debugging script on the client and server side. We will also investigate how this affects system performance and how we can streamline our code to make the best use of instance resources.

10
Best Practices

In this chapter, we will be looking at best practices when scripting in ServiceNow. Best practices are important when scripting to make the most use of resources and present the best user experience. We will explore best practices in general scripting, server-side and client-side code, and debugging. We will also delve into best practices involving logs, queues, and system performance.

The following topics will be looked at in this chapter:

- Coding best practices
- Business rule best practices
- Client script best practices
- Debugging tools best practices
- Logs and queues best practices
- System performance best practices

Coding best practices

When scripting, there are many ways to achieve the same goal, but keeping code efficient can make it much easier to maintain and work on in the future. Using a few system resources is usually encouraged too, as this decreases loading times and the load on the data center in the cloud.

You will often find that older instances suffer from poor performance because best practices were not adhered to during development. I have been part of minor projects simply to make code more efficient before, and because these are often associated with slow loading times, it can be a great improvement for the user base.

In this section, we will look at how to make sure your script adhers to best practices and how to avoid common mistakes.

First, one type of scripting that is quite common is nested `if` statements. This is an `if` statement after an `if` statement and is often used to catch several potential values for the same variable. We can see a server-side example of what this looks like:

```
var state = current.state;
if (state == '1') {
  gs.log('State is New');
} else if (state == '2') {
  gs.log('State is In Progress');
} else if (state == '6') {
  gs.log('State is Resolved');
}
```

We can also see what this looks like in a script field in *Figure 10.1*:

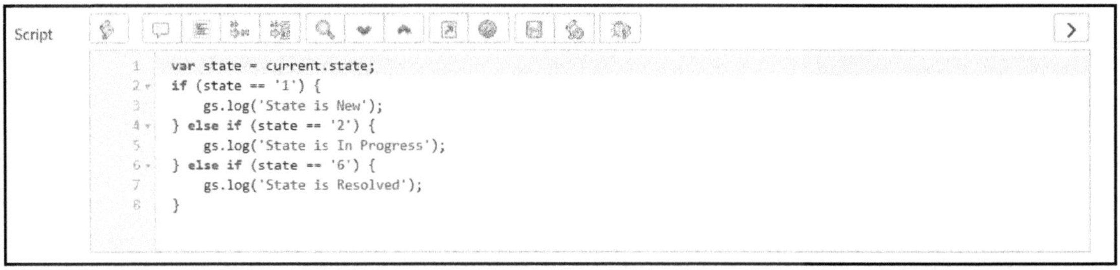

Figure 10.1: Nested if statement script example

Instead of using these nested if statements, it is better to use a `switch` statement. We can see how the previous script can be a more efficient `switch` statement instead:

```
switch(state.getDisplayValue()) {
    case 'New':
    gs.log('State is New');
    break;
    case 'In Progress':
    gs.log('State is In Progress');
    break;
    case 'Resolved':
    gs.log('State is Resolved');
    break;
    default:
    gs.log('Not Found');
}
```

The `switch` statement is easier to read as well for developers who may need to maintain the ServiceNow instance.

We can see the `switch` statement inside a script field in *Figure 10.2*:

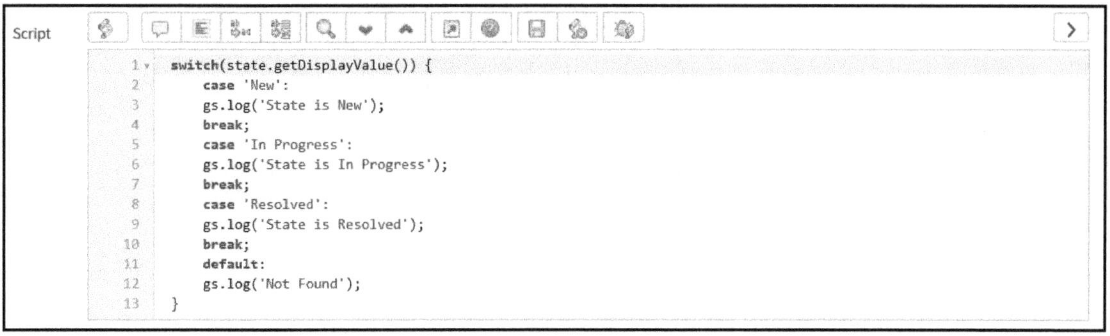

```
switch(state.getDisplayValue()) {
    case 'New':
    gs.log('State is New');
    break;
    case 'In Progress':
    gs.log('State is In Progress');
    break;
    case 'Resolved':
    gs.log('State is Resolved');
    break;
    default:
    gs.log('Not Found');
}
```

Figure 10.2: Switch statement script example

Ensure that you use a break at the end of each case to ensure that the `switch` statement works correctly, as sometimes this can be omitted by mistake.

Business rule best practices

Business rule best practices are, to a large extent, about running business rules at the correct time. As we have already discovered, a business rule can be run at different times based on when the form is saved or the action is taken to the record.

This means that it is important to make sure that a business rule that is created is running in the most efficient way. Using business rules correctly, we can avoid problems such as updating the same record twice and running script when it is not required.

We'll start with looking at the check boxes on a business rule, as shown in *Figure 10.3*:

Figure 10.3: Business rule check boxes

Insert and **Update** are the most frequently used, and they are often used together. However, it is a best practice to ensure that you make your business rule only run when necessary. Do not tick both boxes just to cover all possibilities; if your business rule is not needed when a record is inserted or updated then leave that tick box unchecked.

Usually, **Delete** and **Query** are selected individually, as these operations do not tend to align themselves with any other operations.

As business rules run on the server side, a good practice in business rule script also applies to other areas of ServiceNow where server-side scripting is used.

The **When** field is the next field we will look at. This is an important field to get right, and avoid bad practices by doing so. There are four options here; let's have a look at each.

Before

Running a business rule before a record is saved is a great way to change values before the save action takes place. The before option should be selected when making changes to the record being saved. This means that if you are changing values using current, then before is most likely the best option.

Remember that when running a script in a before business rule, the record has not been saved yet. This means that you only need to set the values in the current record as the record will be saved afterward. This also means that you need to ensure that you avoid using `current.update()` as this will end up saving the record twice.

After

If the business rule is run with the after option selected, the script runs immediately after the record is saved. We should use the after option if we are updating values not on the current record we are saving, but want the script to be run immediately.

This option is useful to update records associated with the record being saved, for example, to change tasks when updating a change. This is also a good option if we are scripting any sort of approval changes for the record being saved, as these will be displayed on the record after it is reloaded, after being saved.

If we are looking to update the current record, then it is better to use the before option. If you are thinking of using `current.update()` in your script, then think about using the before option instead.

Async

The async option will send the script to the system scheduler, and it will be run shortly after the record is saved. This option is good for when the script you have written does not need to be run immediately after the record is saved.

Good uses for the async option are for sending messages between integrations and sending tasks to the ECC queue. Remember that the async option can have a more significant delay if the ServiceNow instance-scheduled job queue is long, so be mindful of the average wait time for your instance when setting an async business rule. If you would like a more instant running of your script, consider the after option.

Display

A display business rule runs when a record is loaded before any client-side scripts are run. This type of business rule is useful for providing values to the client side so that there is no need to call the server from a client script. We can avoid AJAX calls using this type of business rule.

Display business rules were not always available in ServiceNow, so you may find instances where using them in old instances can reduce server calls in client scripts and therefore reduce record-loading times.

If you are considering using an AJAX call in an onLoad client script, then you should instead, where possible, use a display business rule to fetch the server-side values you require and set them in a scratchpad for client-side scripts to use.

Client script best practices

As we have seen, client scripts run on the client side and so only have access to data that has been sent to the client from the server. The main goal we have when writing client-side scripts is to minimize the amount of script we write and the calls to the server we make.

The reason we keep client scripting to a minimum is that these scripts run in front of the user and therefore directly effect loading times. We want to keep loading times to a minimum and, therefore, client scripting to a minimum also.

When writing a new client script, it is worth considering whether the script could be run on the server side instead, and if so, then this is usually considered a best practice.

Let's have a look at one of the most common bad practices in client scripting. Take the following script, for example:

```
function onLoad() {
    var user = new GlideRecord('sys_user');
    user.get(g_form.getValue('caller_id'));
    g_form.showFieldMsg('caller_id', 'Active: ' + user.active);
}
```

This script is calling the server side to get the details about the current caller for an incident, and whether that caller is active now in the system. This is a bad practice as we can already tell whether this user is active before we load the record, rather than loading it, then going back to the database again, increasing load times.

We can see what this code would look like in the following client script:

Figure 10.4: Client script showing bad practise by making an unnecessary server call

To keep this functionality, but improve the code, we can use a display business rule. By doing this, we bring the data we want from the server before we get to the client using a scratchpad.

First, we create the display business rule with the following code:

```
(function executeRule(current, previous /*null when async*/) {

    g_scratchpad.caller_active = current.caller_id.active;

})(current, previous);
```

This code sets the active field value to the `caller_active` scratchpad so that it can be used by the client code.

Let's see what this looks like as a display business rule:

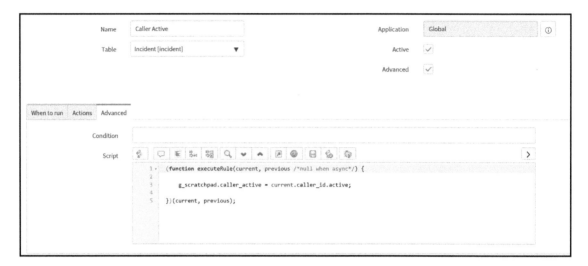

Figure 10.5: Display business rule setting a scratchpad variable

In our business rule, we would set the **When** field on the **When to run** tab to be displayed so that this rule runs as the form is loaded. For our example, we have set the incident form as the table to run this business rule on.

Now, we have the display business rule set up, so we just need to amend our client script:

```
function onLoad() {
  g_form.showFieldMsg('caller_id', 'Active: ' +
g_scratchpad.caller_active);

}
```

In the earlier code, we set the field message text using the scratchpad value we set in the display business rule. This now means that we are not making a round trip to the server for this detail anymore as it is sent initially.

Let's see what this will look like in a defined client script:

Figure 10.6: Client script setting a field message based on a scratchpad value

In our example, we are using the script when the incident form loads. This will show the active state of the caller currently selected on the incident form. We would also want to bear in mind changing this value if the caller changes.

Using this method, we can display any of the other caller attributes as well, including helpful fields like phone number or email address to contact a caller about progress on an incident. We could also display the line manager and use dot walking to display some of the manager's information.

Here, we can see what the output would look like for our example for a caller on the incident form:

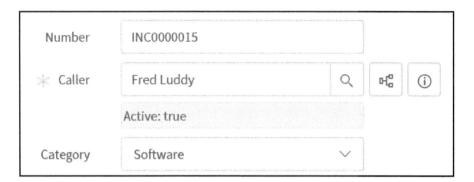

Figure 10.7: Incident form showing a custom field message for the Caller field

We have opened one of the baseline incidents that is present in ServiceNow, and we can see that the current caller is active in ServiceNow.

It is highly recommended to review the client scripts in your ServiceNow instance to ensure that no unnecessary server calls are made by them. Remember to use display business rules where possible.

Debugging tools best practices

As we have discovered in previous chapters, there are many ways to debug in ServiceNow. Each developer will have their own favorite methods, and also, there are better ways to debug different scenarios.

Logging

One of my favorite ways of debugging is using logging techniques such as `gs.log`. In earlier chapters, we saw that these logs can be added to a script, and when the script runs, we see these logs in the system log for the ServiceNow instance.

However, we must ensure that this debugging is never seen in a production instance. It is a good practice to check each script that you write to ensure that no debugging is left in the final version. It can be a good idea to check the system log before your newly created script is executed and then again once you have finished. If there are any logging messages that are sent, then these should be removed before the new functionality is sent to a production instance.

It is also important to make sure that you make your logging messages relevant to the functionality you are trying to achieve. This is especially important if you aim to leave in some logging functionality for your new code. Building some logging functionality can be helpful in a larger application or customization.

Consider, for example, the following code and logging:

```
var caller = current.caller_id;
gs.log('log');
```

This example will create a log when the value of the caller has been successfully put into the caller variable, but it does not offer much information.

We can see the log this creates here:

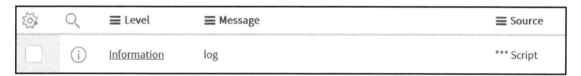

Figure 10.8: Sample basic log

To improve our log, let's look at another example:

```
var caller = current.caller_id;
gs.log('caller id obtained from the caller field');
```

This second example is better because we now have some information about what is happening at this point in the code, and where the code was successful.

The output of this log looks like this:

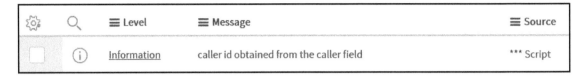

Figure 10.9: Sample improved log

We can still improve this further though by adding more information at this point.

Let's look at a further example on logging in this way:

```
var caller = current.caller_id;
gs.log('caller id obtained from the caller field with value ' + caller);
```

Looking at the example, we now have added code in our logging to log the value of the caller field, as well as the details of what has occurred in the script. This will log the sys_id of the user in the system log, so we can check the value of the caller variable is correct at this point in the code.

We can see this improved log in the following figure:

Figure 10.10: Sample log with data added

Now, we will look at one final example:

```
var caller = current.caller_id;
gs.log('caller id obtained from the caller field with value ' +
caller.getDisplayValue());
```

With this final example, we are now logging the display value to the log, so we can see the actual name of the user rather than just the sys_id of the user. This makes the result clearer for a developer reading through the log statements.

Let's look at how the final example looks in the system log:

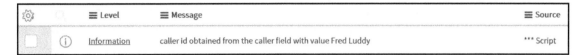

Figure 10.11: Sample log with useful data included

We have seen how it is easy to add logging to ServiceNow script, but it is best practice to ensure that the logs you create would be helpful to developers other than yourself.

Session debug

Session debug can be a powerful tool, but it can also create an overload of logs making debugging a long and arduous process. When using session debugging, it is important to think about the type of logs you need to debug the situation.

While it can seem easiest to simply enable all session debugging, it is best to enable the areas you are interested in only. This ensures there are less logs to go through and means you can access the information that you are interested in faster.

In general, I do not find session debug to be used by many developers except for scopes and security rules. This is because other methods are preferred for the other debugging options session debugging provides.

Logs and queues best practices

Logs and queues are an important part of a ServiceNow instance. Logs are used throughout ServiceNow to record events occurring in an instance. These are used in debugging, as we have seen, and these logs should be well-defined when included.

Queues are seen in ServiceNow in a number of areas, from the ECC queue to the system scheduler. These queues build up jobs or actions to be performed when the time is right.

When using logs and queues, it is important to make logs clear and only create jobs or event in queues where necessary.

Logs

Logs need to be created with clear information given for each log, and to be sent to the right logging location to ensure that the information can be easily read. We covered some logging techniques in the debugging section or how to write good logs, but we also need to make sure that we send logs to the correct log itself.

When using `gs.log`, we can specify a source to send the logs to. If no source is specified, then *** **Script** will be the default source used. This will show the log in the **Script Log Statements** module.

Here, we can see a sample log with the *** **Script** source displayed:

Figure 10.12: Sample script log

If you are creating a larger piece of functionality or a custom application, it is advised that you create your own logging source. By adding your own source, you can keep all of your logging separate and easy to maintain. It is also often the case that a developer will create a module as part of their new application to be directed to logs with the custom source of the application.

Queues

There are many queues in ServiceNow that you can send jobs and events to. Queuing up a task or event allows them to be combined together and processed in a batch rather than individually.

Each queue will be processed after a given time, and the timing that each queue is processed is often set in the system properties. Changing the frequency that a queue is processed will mean that tasks or events are dealt with quicker, but it will have a draining effect on system resources. It is always important to carefully consider this when setting queue processing times at a different value to the defaults that are provided in the baseline system.

Now, let's take a look at some of the most important queues in a ServiceNow instance and the best practice for each queue type.

Event queue

The event queue triggers events that are then picked up by notifications and script actions. Triggering an event does not use many system resources, so volume is not usually a problem. There are many events that are provided and triggered in the baseline system, so this queue will always contain activity.

The more important aspect of setting up scripts to send events to the event queue is making sure that the event is well-defined and only fires when it is supposed to.

Well-explained events are much easier to use for other developers, so try to demonstrate what the event is triggered by in the name of the event itself, and certainly in the definition.

We can see a sample event log here:

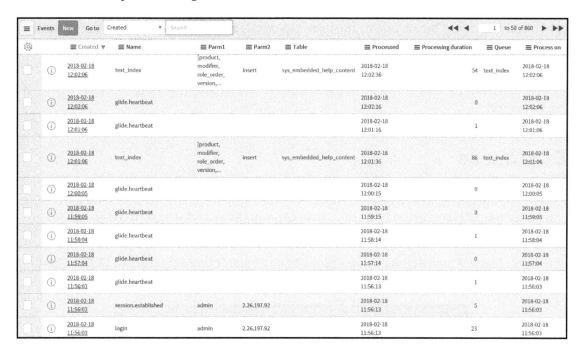

Figure 10.13: Event log sample

In an event log, we can see when events were processed, and the processing duration of events. It is worth considering the impact of events taking a long time to process and, if necessary, investigate why this is the case.

In our example, we can see some regular events in the log including a successful login and established session, as well as a heartbeat event and text indexing.

When creating an event, ensure that you test edge-case scenarios so that the definition of the event truly reflects when it will fire.

 When sending an event to the event queue for the more distant future, be careful that the event will not be lost as part of table rotation.

System scheduler

One of the most common ways that you can add a job to the system scheduler is to use an async business rule. Once an async business rule is triggered, it sends a job to the scheduler queue to run the script contained within it.

It is also possible to add your own jobs to the system scheduler. It is best to only do this where necessary, as too many jobs in the scheduler can be a detriment to instance performance.

ECC queue

The ECC queue is where input and output messages from MID servers are held. This is usually for integrations between instances and other systems. Here, we can send jobs using scripts for the MID servers to perform. There is normally not a lot of scripted messages to the ECC queue as it normally triggers an integration in one line.

The ECC Queue is accessed from the application navigator by navigating to **ECC | Queue**. We can see this module here:

Figure 10.14: ECC queue module

The queue will often contain heartbeat probes sent out to MID servers to check that they are responding. This is done every 5 minutes, and if a response is received, the MID server is marked as up, and if no response is received, the MID server is marked as down.

When sending jobs to the ECC queue, just make sure that each job is relevant and do not send more jobs than are necessary.

System performance best practices

There are a number of attributes that make up the perceived performance of an instance. These can be greatly effected by badly coded scripts or a large number of them that are not required.

One of the most common ways scripting can cause perceived performance delays is when an excess of client scripts are used when a form opens. This causes a big delay in browser rendering and parsing, which is very apparent to the user. As we have mentioned before, a best practice in this scenario is to limit the amount of client scripts created only to those essential, and to ensure that server calls are kept to a minimum.

If information is needed for an `onLoad` client script, then consider a display business rule instead of calling the server from a client script.

Using this method, we can obtain the information we need from the server from the display business rule before displaying a form. Then, we run client-side code in a client script that will be able to use the information we provided from the display business rule.

It is possible to clear the cache of an instance by navigating to your instance name and suffixing it with `/cache.do`. This clears the cache for you and can help when you want to ensure that your new script is being run, and cached data is not being used.

We can see the screen a user is shown when navigating to the page that clears the cache, here in *Figure 10.15*.

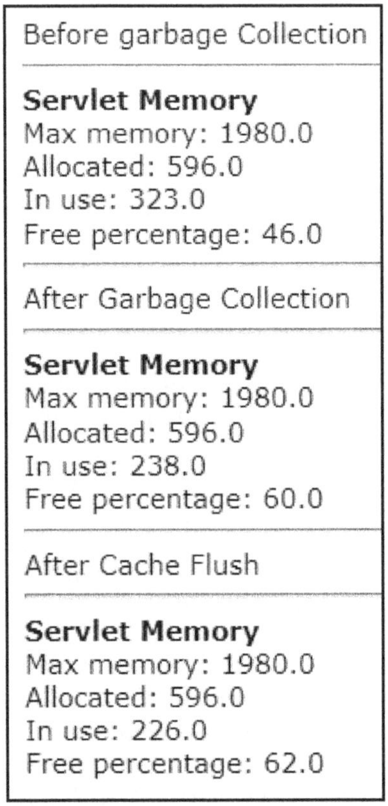

```
Before garbage Collection

Servlet Memory
Max memory: 1980.0
Allocated: 596.0
In use: 323.0
Free percentage: 46.0

After Garbage Collection

Servlet Memory
Max memory: 1980.0
Allocated: 596.0
In use: 238.0
Free percentage: 60.0

After Cache Flush

Servlet Memory
Max memory: 1980.0
Allocated: 596.0
In use: 226.0
Free percentage: 62.0
```

Figure 10.15: Information provided on cache clearance

Clearing the cache for an instance, however, can cause performance degradation, so it is important to know when to do this. On non-production instances, this should not be a problem, as the performance decrease should not dramatically affect other developers. For a production instance though, this should be avoided during business hours where possible.

When considering system performance, it is also worth checking the performance of the instance being used. This can be done using the ServiceNow performance home page that ServiceNow provides.

Let's have a look at some of the graphs that this home page provides:

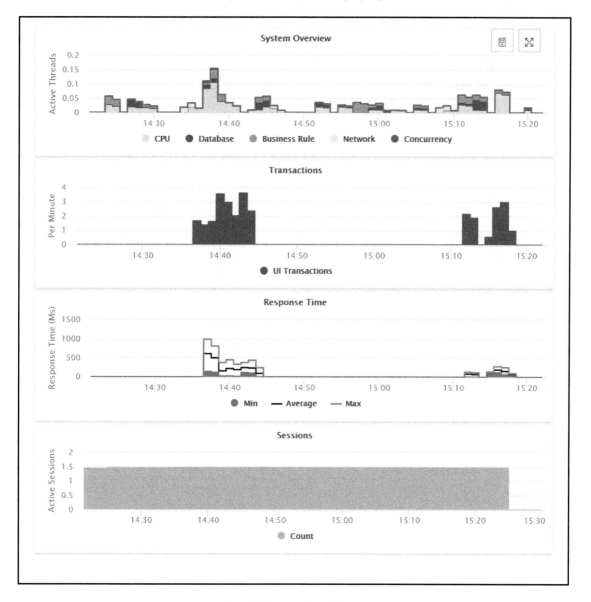

Figure 10.16: System overview graphs sample

In the previously shown graphs, we can see an overview, transaction, response time, and active session graph. These can be helpful in finding out the current load on the instance and whether the response times are providing a good level of service.

The ServiceNow performance home page also displays many other graphs than the ones shown, which you can use. I tend to find the response times the most useful of the ones provided, but each graph can have its uses.

By keeping an eye on instance performance, you can be proactive in resolving potential system performance issues.

Summary

In this chapter, we looked at best practices in ServiceNow. We looked at some of the best ways to use scripting in ServiceNow, and some bad practices to avoid. Our best practices included the areas of coding, business rules, and client scripts, as well as debugging, logs, queues, and system performance. We saw how these best practices work together to build a streamlined ServiceNow instance.

In the next chapter, we will look at using update sets. Update sets are a big part of moving functionality between instances of ServiceNow, and are widely used. We will look at when and how to use update sets and how they work in relation to scope. We discover how to move update sets between instances and the pitfalls to avoid when doing so. Finally, we take a look at best practices with update sets, so you can make the most of the ServiceNow application.

11
Deployments with the Update Sets

In this chapter, we will be looking at how to use update sets. Update sets are a big part of ServiceNow and move new functionality from non-production instances to production instances with minimal risk. We will look at when and how to use update sets, as well as how to use them to transfer functionality from one instance to another. After this, we will explore pitfalls to be avoided and best practices for update sets.

In this chapter, we will look at the following topics:

- When to use update sets
- How to use scope with update sets
- Transferring update sets between instances
- Update set pitfalls
- Update set best practices

When to use update sets

Update sets are used in ServiceNow to move functionality from one instance to another. If you are making some changes in a development instance which you would like to later move to a production instance, then update sets are recommended.

An update set captures changes that you make to an instance, inside the update set, while they are being made. Once all the changes that you would like captured are finished, the update set is complete and is ready to be moved to another instance. When moved to another instance, the update set can be previewed to check that the changes are compatible with the instance and committed to apply the changes.

Before making any changes that you intend to move to another instance, your first task should be to create a new update set to contain those changes. Before you start making changes, ensure that you are working inside the update set. Once the updates are complete, complete the update set that is ready to move to another instance.

How to use scope with update sets

When using update sets, we need to remember what scope we are currently working in. Before we use any kind of scope in an instance, we are in the global scope, and before we create any update sets in an instance, we are in the default update set.

If we are not in a created update set, then we will also be in the default update set. However, there is a different default update set for each scope in a ServiceNow instance. This is important to know so that if you do switch scopes, then your update set automatically changes, as well.

We can see this change in the update set picker if we change the scope we are working on in an instance. In *Figure 11.1*, we can see an instance in the **Global** scope:

Figure 11.1: Application and update set picker in the global scope

Because we are in the **Global** scope, the default update set selected for us is the default update set for the **Global** scope. We can see that this is shown to us by the ServiceNow instance by the text inside the square brackets in the update set picker.

If we change only the application, and, therefore, the scope, we can see the change in the update picker, too. Let's change the application to **Guided Setup** as an example, to see the change.

We can see these changes in *Figure 11.2*:

Figure 11.2: Application and update set picker in the guided setup scope

As you can see, the update set is automatically changed for us. This means that there can be a number of different default update sets in an instance, and each application will have its own.

The example brings us nicely on to another point about using update sets in different scopes. Each update set can only exist in a single scope. Before creating an update set, ensure that you are currently in the correct scope, so that changes you make can be added to the update set. Once created, ServiceNow security stops anyone from writing to the application field of an update set. This is set by a security rule and should not be amended.

Transferring update sets between instances

Once an update set has been completed, it is ready to be transferred to another instance. Transferring update sets between instances takes a few steps, and once initially set up, it can be a quick process.

To start the process of moving an update set between two instances, we first need to log in to the instance we want to move the update set to, or the destination instance. Then we navigate to **System Update Sets | Update Sources** and click **New**.

We can see the new update source screen in *Figure 11.3*:

Figure 11.3: New update source form

On this form, there are some key fields to fill in. Let's start with the mandatory fields first: **Name** and **URL**. The **Name** field is exactly that – a name to give to our update source so a system admin can easily recognize this update source. This is often the name of the instance we are taking the update set from, or the source instance. The **URL** field needs to be the URL of the source instance in the format `<instance_name>.service-now.com`.

The other important fields on this form are the **Username** and **Password** fields. These need to be a username and password for the source instance, and the account has to be an admin account for that instance.

The **Type** and **Short description** fields can also be filled in to add extra labels to help identify the update source. Once the form is complete, click **Test connection** to ensure that the source instance can be accessed. If the connection fails, you may need to check the information you provided and make sure the source instance can be accessed and does not have any IP access controls that could be causing a failure.

If the connection is a success, then the form can be saved. Once an update source has been saved, we can then start to bring in update sets from the source instance. A related link called **Retrieve Completed Update Sets** is now available to click. Once this is selected, all completed update sets will be transferred to the destination instance.

> Remember to complete any update sets you want to move to another instance, as incomplete update sets will not be moved.

To see the update sets that have been moved to the destination instance, we can navigate to **System Update Sets** | **Retrieved Update Sets**. Now that the update set exists in the destination instance, we need to apply the customization to the destination instance, too.

The update sets that have been retrieved should have been automatically previewed; however, in older instances, this may not be the case, and it may need to be done manually. Sometimes a preview may bring up some warnings or errors that need to be reviewed before an update set can be committed. This can mean that there are missing tables or that a newer update for a particular customization exists on the destination instance. Most of the time, these errors and warnings still end up with the remote update being accepted and committed, but review each one to ensure you should be committing all the updates.

Once the preview process is complete, you can commit your update set. This will add all of the customizations in the update set from the source instance to the destination instance, excluding any marked to skip as part of the preview process.

When the commit is complete, you have successfully transferred an update set from one instance to another.

Update set pitfalls

Update sets are a great way to move configurations between instances. However, when using update sets, there are some pitfalls that can easily be fallen into.

The main issue that most developers face is what customization will be added to an update set. Not all changes to tables are added to update sets. Whether changes to a table are added to an update set or not depends on whether the records in the table are considered data or not. Tables that are considered as data are not added to an update set; as otherwise, update sets would be filled with unnecessary records.

For example, if the incident table was included in update sets, any incidents modified or created in a development instance would be moved across to a production instance, which would not be a good idea. Most tables are included or excluded from update sets as you would expect, but some are not always obvious, so it is worth checking.

To avoid missing updates in our update sets or including updates we do not want, we can check to see which tables we are working with and send updates to an update set. To do this, we can look at the dictionary entry of the table we are working with.

From the list of dictionary entries for a table, we are interested in the record with a type of **Collection**. This gives the definition of the table and also holds the attributes for the table, which is what we need to look at. The attribute that adds updates to a table to update sets is called **Update synch**, and it needs to be **true**. Usually, if this attribute has been added it will be set to **true**, and if it is omitted then it will be **false**.

Let's have a look at the dictionary entry for the incident table shown in *Figure 11.4*:

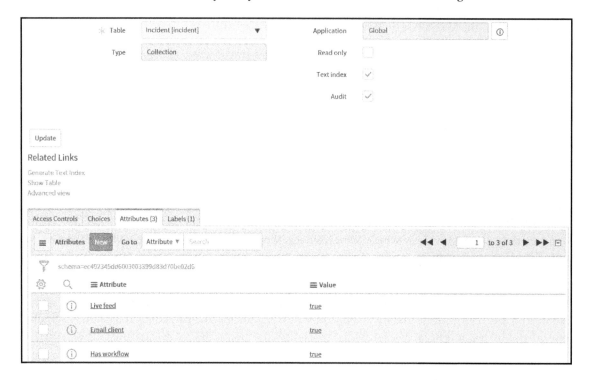

Figure 11.4: Dictionary entry for the incident table

As the incident table holds incident data, we do not want incident records in our update sets. As we can see, the **Update synch** attribute does not appear here, so any incidents we create or modify will not end up in the update set.

Now let's see the dictionary entry for client scripts. We can see this in *Figure 11.5*:

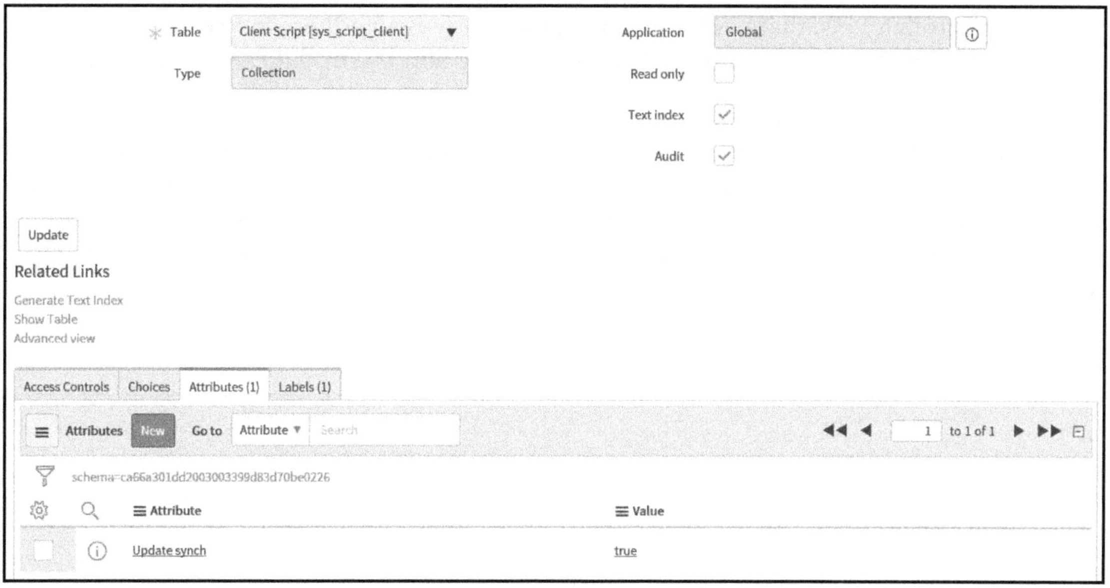

Figure 11.5: Dictionary entry for the client script table

In the **Attributes** of the client script dictionary entry, we can see the **Update synch** attribute, and it is set to **true**. This means that client script records will be added to update sets.

One table that is not included in update sets that is often assumed to be included is the scheduled job table. Because most records containing script are added to update sets, this can often catch developers out. A scheduled job can be moved by exporting it to XML and importing it into another instance.

In contrast, the table that many developers do not realize will be added to update sets is the System Properties table. Sometimes settings for developer instances, such as notifications set up to stop notifications being sent out, can end up being transferred to a production instance by mistake. This is a pitfall I have seen a few times over the years.

Update set best practices

When using update sets, there are some best practices we can adhere to to ensure we avoid adding bad customizations to our production instance and use update sets to their full potential.

Firstly, it is always a good idea to check the updates contained in your update set before completing it. Sometimes a developer can inadvertently add an update they did not mean to to their update set. Therefore, it is always a good idea to check each individual update contained in your update set. In particular, pay special attention to any updates where the action is DELETE, as this can be harder to undo.

We can see some example updates in an update set in *Figure 11.6*:

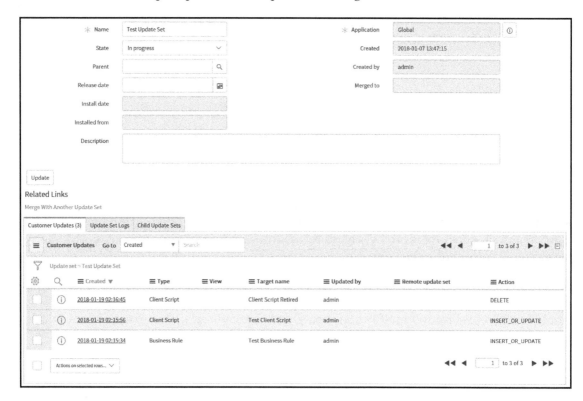

Figure 11.6: Update set containing sample updates

We can see the updates in this update set in the **Customer Updates** tab of the related lists. We can see three updates in the update set example, including two client scripts and a business rule. We need to ensure that every customer update we see is a change we want to include in this update set, and no additional updates have been included in this update set by mistake.

In the **Action** column, the action that will be taken when this update set is committed is shown. Of the three updates, we want to pay special attention to the one with the **DELETE** action to ensure this action does indeed need to be taken. Once a record is deleted, it can be more difficult to undo the action. An insert or update is a much easier update to change or revert to an earlier version.

It is also a good idea to have a naming convention for your update sets. At first ,when update sets are small in number, this seems unnecessary; but as an instance matures and the number of update sets grows, it can be extremely helpful. The naming convention does not need to be complex, just consistent. Common naming conventions can be for releases, sprints, or the record number of stories or defects.

Some examples of naming conventions are:

- Description - Release - Date
- Story/Defect: Developer
- Sprint/Month

When deciding on a naming convention, decide on the details that are relevant for your process and instance, and make sure the convention is adhered to.

As we saw earlier in this chapter, when setting up an update source, we need to provide a username and password for an admin account for the instance we are taking update sets from. It is good practice to ensure the account details used for the update source are for an account that will not be amended frequently, as this will stop the update source from being able to pull update sets from that instance.

With update sets, it is good practice to ensure that update sets being committed in a production instance are done so at an appropriate time. As with any change to a production system, there is a level of risk associated. This means committing update sets should be done outside of business hours if possible, or at least at a quiet period of time, in case any problems arise.

Summary

We looked at update sets in this chapter. We saw how to use update sets and how they are used with different application scopes. In this chapter, we also explored transferring update sets between instances, avoiding pitfalls for update sets, and best practices when using update sets, especially when checking each update set update.

In the final chapter, we will use all that we have learned to build a custom application in ServiceNow. We will look at how to create a custom application and, specifically, how to use script in a custom application. We will discover end-to-end development of a custom application, as well as how to test and deploy the custom application we have made.

12
Building a Custom Application Using ServiceNow Scripting

In this final chapter, we will be looking at building a custom application using ServiceNow scripting. Custom applications are a great way to create functionality not included with the ServiceNow product. We will be looking at creating a custom application and using scripting as part of our application. We will also learn about end-to-end creation of a custom application before exploring how to test and deploy our new custom application.

In this chapter, we will be looking at the following topics:

- Creating a custom application with ServiceNow scripting
- End-to-end development
- Testing
- Deployment

Creating a custom application with ServiceNow scripting

The ability to build a custom application in ServiceNow makes ServiceNow such a versatile product. As ServiceNow was first released to the market as a service desk solution, developers have explored the potential of the platform, and since then it has been used in various areas of the business.

However, there are still many ways of using ServiceNow that are not included with the baseline system, and for this, we can create a custom application.

Before creating a custom application, it is worth considering whether a custom application will provide the best solution. Sometimes, we can use an existing ServiceNow application to perform the functionality we want to achieve, using it directly or slightly modifying it for our needs. If this is the case, then it is worth considering not creating a custom application and using the platform instead.

If the functionality you need would take a large modification to an existing application or simply does not exist at that point, it is advisable to create a custom application.

Creating the application

Once we create a new application, we can then start adding application files to that application. The application files we create become part of the application.

To create a new application, we can navigate to **System Applications** | **Applications**, and we will be shown the current applications that have been created on this instance. We then need to click on the **New** button on the far right, as shown in *Figure 12.1*:

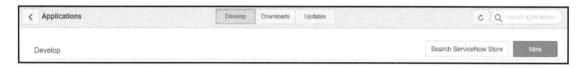

Figure 12.1: Instance applications page

Once the **New** button has been selected, you are given a series of choices about where you would like to start from when creating your application.

We can see the options given in *Figure 12.2*:

Figure 12.2: Application creation options

From this set of choices, we can decide from what starting point we want to create our application. The top two choices are the most commonly used generally. Starting from scratch is exactly that, only the application is created and the new application scope. No tables or modules or access controls are made for you.

Creating a custom application guides you through creating a table, modules, and access controls. After that, it is much the same as starting from scratch.

The third option, to start from a service, is rarely used in my experience, but allows a developer to enhance a service created from the service creator and potentially overwrite it when complete.

The final option here is not available as part of the baseline system, but can be used if service management is activated. This option again is not as well used, although it allows creation from an existing process.

When selecting start from a template, we are presented with a further page, which we can see in *Figure 12.3*:

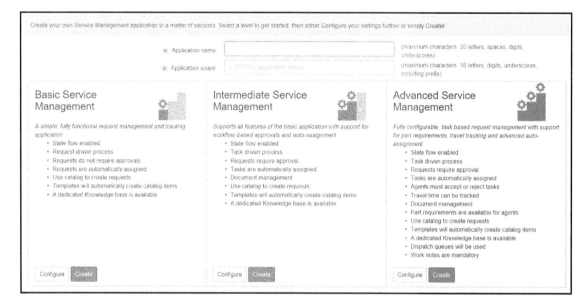

Figure 12.3: Application creation template option choices

From here, we can either create from a predefined template, or configure settings further to create the application.

Now the custom application has been created, we can start to add application files and build up the application.

Building the application

Once the application has been created, we can start to build up the application with application files. These are the files that, when put together, make up the application. When the application is created, an application scope is also created for the application. On the creation of the application, you will also be put into the new application scope, so it is important to be aware of this.

You will also see that your update set has changed once you create a new update set to a new default update set for the application scope you are now in. As you are in the application scope of your new application, any customizations made will be added to your new application.

To keep track of the current scope and update set, it can be useful to show the application and update set picker when developing. These two options can be set in the **Developer** tab of the system settings, which can be seen in the following figure:

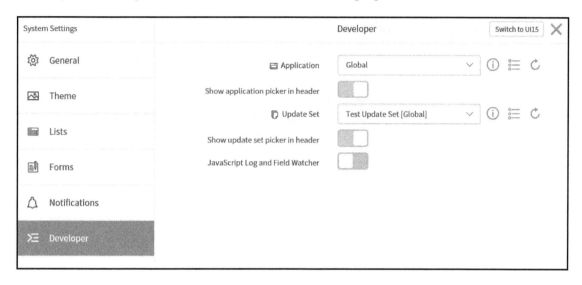

Figure 12.4: Developer system settings showing the application and update set picker

By setting the two picker options in *Figure 12.4*, we are then shown the current application scope and update set at the top of the screen in the header bar. These are shown in a drop-down field, so both can easily be changed if required.

We can see here both of the picker drop-down fields that are displayed in the header bar:

Figure 12.5: Application and update set picker

These picker fields are especially helpful if you are working between update sets or in multiple scopes for your current development.

When working in multiple tabs, it can be a wise idea to refresh your browser page to ensure that the pickers are up-to-date on the tab you are working on.

Now that we have created and started to build our application, we can move on to the development of our application.

Example application

In this chapter, we will also build an example custom application to reinforce the theory that we learn. For our example, we will build an application to hold data for users' access.

First, we need to create the application. From the options we saw in *Figure 12.2*, we are going to select **Create custom application**. Once we have selected this, we are given the form shown in *Figure 12.6*:

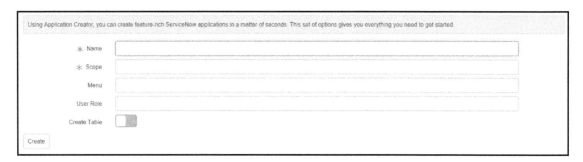

Figure 12.6: Create custom application form

In this form, we need to give our application a name, which will then fill in the rest of the fields. We can change the values in the fields, but in the **Scope** field, the prefix will have to be the prefix for your company or developer instance.

For our example, we also want to create a table, so we'll need to check the **Create Table** option too. This gives us some extra table fields to fill in. These will be populated for you, but you can change them to fit your needs.

Here, we can see the filled-in form for our user access application. Custom application prefixes start with x_ and are followed by the prefix specific to you or your company. This scope is mandatory, and specific to you. The blank spaces in *Figure 12.7* are where this prefix would be shown:

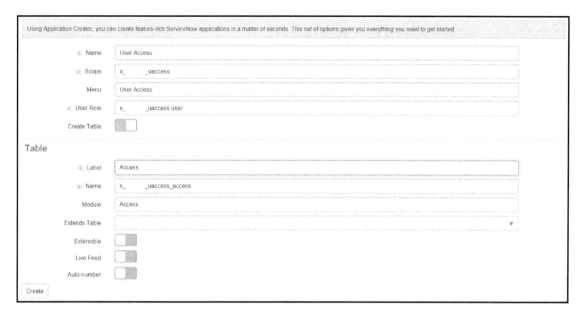

Figure 12.7: Completed custom application form

Now we have completed the form, we click on the **Create** button at the bottom of the form.

We are given a confirmation popup before the application and new table are created, which we can see here:

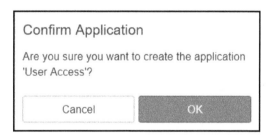

Figure 12.8: Custom application creation confirmation popup

For our example, we will click on **OK** and create the application. Once the application is created, we are given a button to edit the application that opens up the development studio, which we will explore more in the next section.

We have successfully created our application and will pick up our user access application example in the next section.

End-to-end development

Once an application has been created on an instance, we can move on to developing the application. When we are in the application scope of our application, all customizations are added to the application. We can either make changes to the instance in the same way we usually would do development outside of an application, for example, creating and amending scripts, or we can use the studio ServiceNow provides for us.

Studio

The studio was created by ServiceNow for use when creating custom applications. Some developers prefer the studio, as it shows the application in one place, whereas others prefer to develop as they would in the global scope.

To access the studio, navigate to **System Applications** | **Studio**. This will open a new tab in your browser and give us the opportunity to load one of the applications that have been created on the current instance.

We can see the **Load Application** form in *Figure 12.9*:

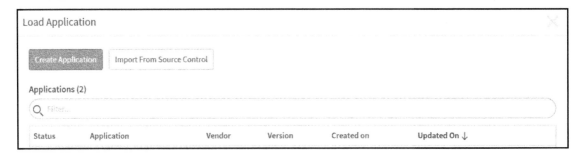

Figure 12.9: Studio load application form

In the list, you will see the applications available to load on the instance you are working in. Once we have loaded the application we want to work on in the studio, we can see the current application files on the left-hand side. We can see the screen show in *Figure 12.10*:

Figure 12.10: Sample studio for a test application

As an example, a business rule and client script have been created for this test application.

When we have a new application, we need to create a new application file to start. To create a new application file, we can click on the **Create Application File** button we can see in the preceding figure.

We are then given the **Create Application File** screen, shown in *Figure 12.11*, where we can select what type of application file we want to create in our application:

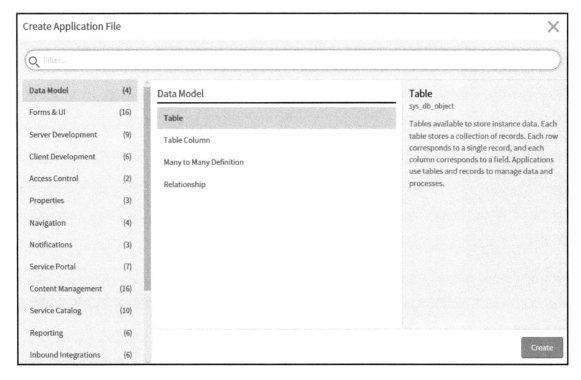

Figure 12.11: Application file creation screen

There are many application file types to choose from, with some of the more common being client scripts, business rules, access controls, and tables. Once the application file has been selected, click **Create** to start editing the application file. Once the application file is finished and saved, it will appear in the left-hand pane of the studio.

One of the main benefits of using the studio is that you can keep track of all the application files in the left-hand pane very easily and amend them by clicking on them. Another big benefit is the ability to use tabs to quickly flick between different application files. We can see this in *Figure 12.12*:

Figure 12.12: Studio tabbed development example

As you can see from the preceding figure, we can have many tabs open for different application files. This can be for new or existing application files, and is certainly one of the features I like about using Studio.

Studio is very good for collating all of the aspects of an application together, but whether to use it or not is the developer's preference. Some developers swear by it, others will not use it at all, and some developers are somewhere in between.

Application development

Whether using studio or not, once an application is created, we need to do the development and make sure that all of the application files we need for our application are created. Each application is different, and the ability to create unique applications in ServiceNow is almost limitless.

When developing your application, remember the skills and techniques we have covered in the earlier chapters of this book to get the best out of it.

When creating a new application, I would recommend considering the table structure of the application first and associated relationships. Once the table structure is in place, the other application files will be easier to plan and place into the application.

ServiceNow also allows us to add records considered as data to our custom applications. This allows us to take across records where the **Update sync** attribute we discovered in the previous chapter is not set to true for the table. To do this, we can right-click on the header bar for a list view, and we are given the option to **Create Application Files**, as shown in *Figure 12.13*:

Figure 12.13: Creating application files from a list view

In *Figure 12.13*, we are looking at an incident list with only one record in the list due to the filter. On selecting the **Create Application Files** option, we will then be given a popup to select how the application files should be added. This popup can be seen in *Figure 12.14*:

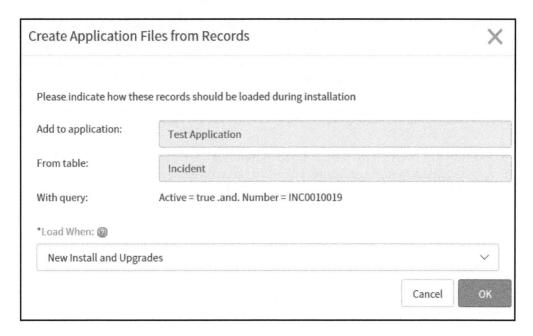

Figure 12.14: Creating application files popup

This popup in *Figure 12.14* has a field of **Load When**, and this is the most important field on this form. From here, we have the following three options that we can choose:

- **New Install and Upgrades**
- **New Install**
- **New Install with Demo Data**

The first two options are quite straightforward: the data is either loaded only with a new installation of the application and never again, or with a new installation and for future upgrades of the application. The third option is slightly different, but the concept of demo data will be familiar to most system admins. With this option, the records will be available to add when the application is deployed, although it is not mandatory. When we discuss deployment later on in the chapter, the options around including demo data will become clear.

Once a selection has been made for the **Load When** field, we can click on **OK**, and the records will be added to our application. We can see what that looks like for our test application and our previous example in *Figure 12.15*:

Figure 12.15: Sample application files shown included in an application related list

In *Figure 12.15*, we can see that the incident record that was showing in our list view has been moved into the application files of our custom application.

After all of the application files needed for your application have been added, we can then move to testing the application.

Example application

Now we have had a look at how to develop our applications, we can develop our example application too. Our example application user access has been created, and we can either develop in the usual way or use the studio to create new application files from.

From simply creating our application, we will already see some application files as part of our application, which will show in the studio or in the application definition.

We can now see what our application looks like in the studio in the following figure:

Figure 12.16: Studio for user access application

We can already see that, by creating our application, we have a table, role, some access controls, an application menu, and modules. These have all been created in our application scope.

Now we need to create another table to act in a similar way to a many-to-many relationship table between user and access. We could create an m2m table, but we will just create a normal table this time around as we do not want an **Edit** button in the related list between the tables. We can create this table by navigating to **System Definition | Tables & Columns** and clicking on **Create Table** in the usual way, and it will be added to the application too.

We have two tables we need now, so we will add some reference fields to the **User Access** table for **User** and **Access**. The access field links to our other new application table.

We can see what the form looks like, now with some dummy data in it, in *Figure 12.17*:

Figure 12.17: User access custom table form view

We also need to add a **Name** field to our access table, so we can identify each access item, and we'll add a related list to see all users with that access too.

We can see what this form looks like now, again with some dummy data, as follows:

Figure 12.18: Access custom table form view

The table structure for our **User Access** application is now complete. There are now three tables that will be used in the application, which are the user table, supplied with baseline ServiceNow, the access table, and the user access table.

We have created a way of keeping track of the access each user has in ServiceNow. It is generally a good practice to do the table structure of a custom application first, as any scripts or relationships are then easier to plan for the application. Having to add tables later in the application can cause problems or a significant amount of rework in the case of some applications.

We also want to make sure that once a user has been given access in our application, we stop that user being selected for the same access, which means creating a scripted advanced reference qualifier.

First, we will add some script in an advanced reference qualifier to call a script include for us. This reference qualifier will be for the **User** field on the **User Access** table:

```
javascript:new userAccessRefQual().stopDuplicateUserAccess(current.access);
```

Now we have the reference qualifier calling a script include, and we need to create the script include and input code to return only the users without the currently selected access.

Our script include code will look like this:

```
var userAccessRefQual = Class.create();
userAccessRefQual.prototype = {
    initialize: function() {
    },
    /* Returns users that do not currently have this access
    variables:
    access - sys_id of the current access
    */
    stopDuplicateUserAccess: function(access) {
      var usersWithAccess = [];
      var accessRec = new GlideRecord('x_152110_uaccess_user_access');
      accessRec.addQuery('access', access);
      accessRec.query();
      while (accessRec.next()) {
        usersWithAccess.push(accessRec.user.toString());
      }
      return 'sys_idNOT IN' + usersWithAccess.toString();
    },

    type: 'userAccessRefQual'
};
```

This code will check all of the current user access records with the currently selected access from the form and ensure that the users returned to be selected are users that do not currently have this access.

This is done by returning the string `sys_idNOT IN` and the contents of the array that has been populated with all of the users that currently have access to the current access on the form. This can be a very helpful technique to filter out all records we do not want, to only leave the records we do that to be displayed to the user.

We can see the script include created in the following figure:

Figure 12.19: Script include providing advanced reference qualifier functionality

Now that we have our script complete and our tables in place, we are happy to complete our application development-wise. There are certainly further additions we could make to this application to enhance it, like adding extra validation, scripts, or fields to the tables, but we will finish the application at this point for our example.

Testing

A big part of any custom application is testing it to make sure that it functions correctly. Applications with errors or poor functionality can quickly leave customers disillusioned with the application, and often the application will then not be used. Therefore, it is extremely important that any application is thoroughly tested before it is deployed.

When testing a new custom application, it is important to also test around the application as well as the application itself. This means do not just test that the application works, also test that any applications the new application is linked or related to also still functions in the way it did before. This is particularly important when dealing with access controls and security, and always ensure that no access is granted that should not be and that existing users of an application are not locked out of data they had access to before.

If we do come across issues when performing our testing, it is worth remembering the techniques that we learned in the Chapter 9, *Debugging the Script*, with regard to debugging applications. We can use the session debugging tools, including debugging scopes, to fix any problems we encounter.

There is also the option of the following scoped application logging levels to fix issues:

- Error
- Warn
- Info
- Debug

These logs can be important for finding out where problems lie, and remember that gs.log will not work in a custom application scope.

It is a good practice to check the system logs when testing your custom application, to ensure that no logging messages have been left in that should not have been. We need to ensure that these logging messages do not get deployed into a production instance if they are not required.

Example application

Now that the development is complete, for our example application, we will look at testing it. The main aspect of our application we need to look at is the script we created.

However, it is always important to check every aspect of your application, especially against the requirements of the stakeholders that the application will be for.

Some dummy data has been added so that we can check our script is working correctly in the user access and access tables. The **User** table is populated with users in the ServiceNow baseline system that you can use when testing applications.

We can see the entries in the **User Access** table in the following figure:

Figure 12.20: User access custom table list view

As can be seen in *Figure 12.20*, there are two users that have access to **Server A100**. This means that if we try to select these users when **Server A100** is selected, we should not be able to pick those users.

Let's check if this is possible or not:

Figure 12.21: User access custom table form testing the User field reference qualifier

As we can see in the previous figure, after searching for `Fred`, we do not see `Fred Luddy`, which is a good sign and it tells us that our scripted reference qualifier is working correctly.

As part of testing, we will also remove the access to **Server A100** from `Fred Luddy` and check that he is then available for selection when creating a user access records for **Service A100**. With the code we have created, this test also passes and meets the requirements.

There are further tests you can perform, and the level of testing a developer undertakes is often dependent on a number of variables. This can include the impact of the new application on current applications, and whether testing is performed by a separate testing team or not. We will complete testing for our example user access application here.

When testing your applications, choose a level of testing suitable for your needs, and remember to test edge cases if you think that they may bring about testing failures.

Deployment

Once all of the testing has been completed, we can then move on to deploying our custom application to other instances. We can deploy our custom application once we have completed it in the following three main ways:

- Publish the application to an update set
- Publish to the application repository
- Publish to the ServiceNow store

Let's have a look at how to deploy using each method.

Publish to an update set

The first method we will look at is how to publish the custom application to an update set. This is a very helpful method as this allows the update set to be sent to other instances as a retrieved update set, or even exported and imported on any ServiceNow instance. This makes this method of deployment arguably the most versatile.

To publish a custom application to an update set, we first need to navigate to the application record. To do this, we can navigate to **System Applications | Applications** and then click on the name of the application. Make sure not to click on edit as this will open the studio instead.

Under the related links menu, click on the option to **Publish to Update Set...** and then the following screen will be shown:

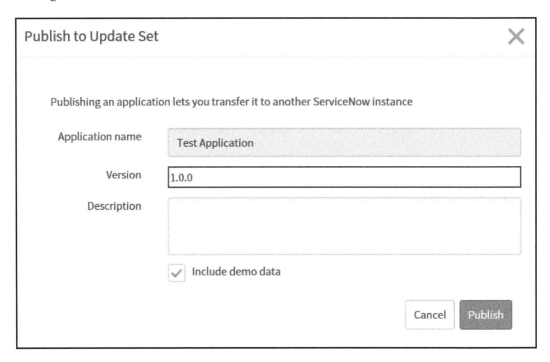

Figure 12.22: Publish to update set popup

In our example, we see the **Test Application** name, but your custom application name will appear here. Enter a **Version**, and it is recommended to add a **Description**, so users will know the function of your application. We saw how we can add data files to our application as demo data earlier in the chapter. The final checkbox allows that demo data to be included in or excluded from the update set we create.

Once the pop-up form is complete, a progress bar will appear:

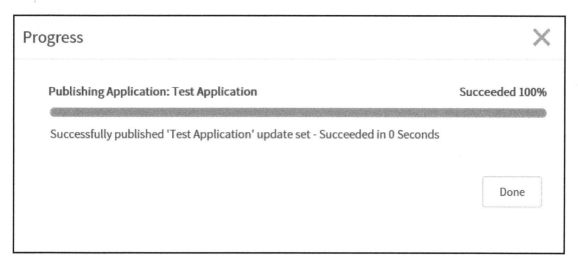

Figure 12.23: Publishing application progress bar

Click on the **Done** button once the publishing completes, and you will be redirected to the update set that has been created. The update set is created at a complete state, so it is ready to be retrieved from other instances immediately. Remember that it is also possible to export the update set to XML.

Now, the application is contained in a completed update set, it can be easily moved between instances.

Publish to the application repository

Next, we look at how to publish our custom application to the application repository. The application repository is company-wide, and it allows easy movement of new custom applications and upgrades between instances in the same company.

First, we need to navigate to the **Application Record**. To do this, we can navigate to **System Applications | Applications** and then click on the name of the application again.

In the related links, click on the link **Publish to My Application Repository**. Follow through the process in a similar way to publishing into an update set, and the application will then be available in the application repository for all of the other instances associated with the current instance company.

We can then install the application on a different instance in the same company by navigating to **System Applications** | **Applications** and clicking on the **Downloads** tab. From here, we should see the application that we sent to the repository displayed with the option to install.

Once the application has been installed, updates made to the application in the instance where the application was created will also be available to other instances for the specific company, if they are added to the repository as the application was.

Publish to the ServiceNow store

The final deployment method we will explore is to publish an application to the ServiceNow store. The ServiceNow store is a way for developers to create custom applications that are then sold through the ServiceNow store to companies looking for that functionality in their instance. Applications can be sold for a one-off fee, monthly subscription, or through consultancy with the developing company.

To be able to publish applications to the ServiceNow store, the company must be a technology partner of ServiceNow, so this option will not be available in all instances.

To begin the process, we again navigate to **System Applications** | **Applications** and then click on the name of the application. Once we have the application record open, we click on the related link **Publish to ServiceNow Store**. This packages up the code in the application into a staging area that can be edited before publishing.

Publishing an application to the ServiceNow store is quite an involved process, which requires ServiceNow to review the application itself and the relevant documentation about the application. We have explored how to start the process here, but once the process has been started, ServiceNow will guide you through the requirements from a developer to take an application into the ServiceNow store.

Example application

Our user access example application is now complete, having been developed and tested. We will now need to deploy the application to other ServiceNow instances.

For our example, we will choose the method of publishing to an update set so that we could take this application to any ServiceNow instance. As we learned earlier in this section, we need to open up the user access application and click on the related link **Publish to Update Set...** to start.

In the window that appears, we fill in the form as shown here:

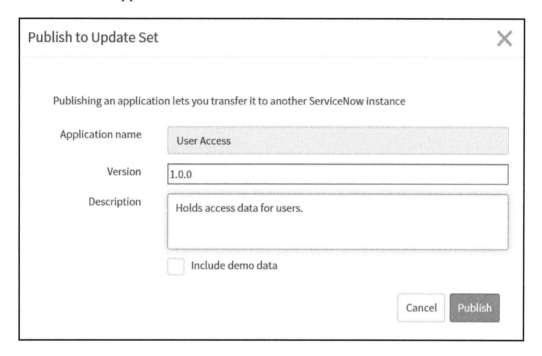

Figure 12.24: Publish to update set popup for user access application

We do not have demo data for our user access application, so we can uncheck the box. A description has also been added to let administrators who install the application know what functionality the application can provide.

Once the **Publish** button is clicked, we can then see the new update set once the process has completed. This update set is already set to **Complete** when is is created.

We can see the update set created for our application here:

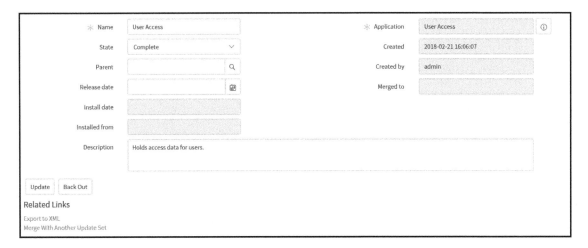

Figure 12.25: Update set for published custom application user access

The update set for our application can now be exported to XML using the related link, which will then allow the application to be imported into any other ServiceNow instance.

To import the update set into another instance, a system administrator can simply import the XML by right-clicking the header bar of a list view and selecting **Import XML**. The update set will then be available to be previewed and committed.

It is also possible to set up or use an existing update source to pull this completed update set into another ServiceNow instance you have.

Using our user access application example, we have seen the various stages of custom application development and how to progress through each stage. ServiceNow is such an open-ended platform that the custom applications that can be created are almost limitless.

Summary

In this final chapter, we looked at how to build a custom application. We looked at how to create a new custom application and the different starting points available. The end-to-end development of a custom application was looked into, including the use of studio. We finished by delving into how to test and deploy a custom application once development is complete.

Through this chapter, we have also seen how to take an example user access application through all of the stages of creating a custom application. From creation to development and then to testing, we finally created an update set containing our application for deployment on other ServiceNow instances.

Building a custom application is a great learning experience and a fantastic way to practice the techniques we have covered in this book. I hope that you enjoy being creative and creating some custom applications of your own.

Other Books You May Enjoy

If you enjoyed this book, you may be interested in these other books by Packt:

ServiceNow Application Development

Sagar Gupta

ISBN: 978-1-78712-871-2

- Customize the ServiceNow dashboard to meet your business requirements
- Use Administration and Security Controls to add roles and ensure proper access
- Manage tables and columns using data dictionaries
- Learn how application scopes are defined within ServiceNow
- Configure different types of table to design your application
- Start using the different types of scripting options available in ServiceNow
- Design and create workflows for task tables
- Use debugging techniques available in ServiceNow to easily resolve script-related issues
- Run scripts at regular time intervals using the Scheduled Script Execution module

Learning ServiceNow

Tim Woodruff

ISBN: 978-1-78588-332-3

- Acquire and configure your own free personal developer instance of ServiceNow
- Read (and write!) clear, effective requirements for ServiceNow development
- Avoid common pitfalls and missteps that could seriously impact future progress and upgradeability
- Know how to troubleshoot when things go wrong using debugging tools
- Discover developer "tips and tricks"
- Pick up great tips from top ServiceNow development and administration professionals, and find out what they wish they knew when they were starting out

Leave a review - let other readers know what you think

Please share your thoughts on this book with others by leaving a review on the site that you bought it from. If you purchased the book from Amazon, please leave us an honest review on this book's Amazon page. This is vital so that other potential readers can see and use your unbiased opinion to make purchasing decisions, we can understand what our customers think about our products, and our authors can see your feedback on the title that they have worked with Packt to create. It will only take a few minutes of your time, but is valuable to other potential customers, our authors, and Packt. Thank you!

Index